AF480911

Navigating Physiology

A Student's Companion

(As per new NCISM Syllabus for 1st Professionals)

(200+ Multiple Choice Question (MCQ) Included)

Dr. Anirudh Sharma
(B.A.M.S, M.D Scholar)

Dr. Apeksha Gautam
(B.A.M.S, M.D)

Navigating Physiology : A Student's Companion

Made with ♥ on the Notion Press Platform

www.notionpress.com

Preface

The journey of understanding physiology is one of uncovering the intricate mechanisms that govern life itself. For students of BAMS, this exploration bridges the ancient wisdom of Ayurveda with modern biomedical science, creating a holistic approach to health and healing. This book, *Navigating Physiology: A Student's Companion*, has been meticulously crafted to align with as per new NCISM 1st year professionals curriculum while providing clarity and depth in its subject matter.

Physiology forms the cornerstone of medical education, offering insights into the normal functioning of the human body and serving as the foundation for understanding pathology and therapeutics. As authors, we have endeavoured to present this complex subject in a student-friendly format, ensuring that it is both accessible and engaging. The chapters have been structured systematically, incorporating diagrams, flowcharts, and real-world examples to make the concepts memorable and practical.

This book is not merely a compilation of facts but an invitation to think critically, ask questions, and explore the wonders of the human body. By integrating principles from modern physiology with an Ayurvedic perspective, we aim to empower students with a comprehensive understanding that is both scientific and contextual.

We express our gratitude to our mentors, colleagues, and students whose encouragement and feedback have been invaluable in shaping this work. To our readers, we hope this book serves as a reliable companion in your academic journey, igniting your curiosity and deepening your appreciation for the study of physiology.

We welcome your suggestions and feedback to help us improve this work further in future editions.

Warm regards,

Dr. Anirudh Sharma & Dr. Apeksha Gautam

:

Acknowledgements

Writing this book, *Navigating Physiology: A BAMS Student's Guide*, has been a fulfilling and transformative journey, and I am deeply grateful to those who have supported and inspired me along the way.

First and foremost, I express my heartfelt gratitude to my father, **Dr. Uttam Kumar Sharma**, whose wisdom and dedication to the medical field have always been a guiding light in my life. Your encouragement and belief in my abilities have been the foundation of my endeavours.

To my mother, **Dr. Triveni Shastri**, your unwavering support and love have been my greatest source of strength. Your compassionate nature and commitment to knowledge continue to inspire me every day.

A special thanks to my sister, **Anuridhi Sharma**, for her constant encouragement and motivation. Your unwavering faith in me has been a driving force in bringing this book to life.

To my mother in law, **Santosh Gautam**, your love and encouragement have been my greatest source of strength. Your constant belief in my abilities has been a cornerstone of my academic and professional life.

To my wife and co-author, **Dr. Apeksha Gautam**, this book would not have been possible without your invaluable contributions, endless patience, and collaborative spirit. Your dedication, expertise, and love have been integral to this project, and I am honoured to have shared this journey with you.

Finally, I extend my gratitude to all my mentors, colleagues, and students whose insights and feedback have enriched this work. This book is a reflection of their influence, guidance, and inspiration.

Thank you all for being a part of this endeavour and for your unwavering belief in the power of education and exploration.

With deepest appreciation,
Dr. Anirudh Sharma

Acknowledgements

The creation of *Navigating Physiology: A BAMS Student's Guide* has been a deeply rewarding experience, and I would like to take this opportunity to express my heartfelt gratitude to those who have supported and encouraged me throughout this journey.

To my father-in-law, **Dr. Uttam Kumar Sharma**, and my mother-in-law, **Dr. Triveni Shastri**, your wisdom, guidance, and blessings have been invaluable. Your unwavering support has given me the confidence to pursue this endeavour with enthusiasm and dedication.

To my mother, **Santosh Gautam**, your love and encouragement have been my greatest source of strength. Your constant belief in my abilities has been a cornerstone of my academic and professional life.

I am also grateful to my brother, **Ashwini Gautam**, for his encouragement and positivity, and to my sister-in-law, **Anuridhi Sharma**, for her unwavering faith in my efforts. Your support has meant the world to me.

To my husband and co-author, **Dr. Anirudh Sharma**, I am immensely thankful for your collaboration, inspiration, and unwavering partnership. This book is a reflection of our shared vision and dedication, and it has been an honor to work alongside you on this project.

Finally, I extend my heartfelt thanks to everyone who has contributed to my journey, including mentors, colleagues, and students, whose insights and feedback have enriched this work.

With deep gratitude,
Dr. Apeksha Gautam

Table of Contents Page No.

Chapter 1- Physiology Homeostasis.................................1 - 18

1.1 Definition and mechanisms of maintenance of homeostasis..........................1 - 4
1.2 Cell physiology..5 – 7
1.3 Membrane physiology...8 – 10
1.4 Transportation of various substances across cell membrane........................11 – 12
1.5 Resting membrane potential and action potential...................................13 – 14
1.6 Acid -base balance, water and electrolyte balance...................................15 – 16
1.7 Study of basic components of food..17 – 18

Chapter 2- Physiology of Respiratory system.........................19 – 25

2.1 Functional anatomy of respiratory system..19 – 20
2.2 Definition of ventilation, mechanism of respiration, exchange and transport of gases, neural and chemical control of respiration artificial respiration, asphyxia, hypoxia. ....21 - 22
2.3 Introduction to Pulmonary Function Tests. ....23 – 25

Chapter 3- Physiology of Gastrointestinal system...................26 – 43

3.1 Functional anatomy of gastro -intestinal tract.....................................26 – 27
3.2 Mechanism of secretion and composition of different digestive juices............28 – 29
3.3 Functions of salivary glands, stomach, liver, pancreas, small intestine and large intestine in the process of digestion and absorption......................30 – 33
3.4 Movements of the gut (deglutition, peristalsis, defecation) and their control......34 – 35
3.5 Enteric nervous system...36 – 37
3.6 Digestion and metabolism of proteins, fats and carbohydrates......................38 – 39
3.7 Vitamins & Minerals...40 – 43

Chapter 4- Physiology of Nervous System..........................44 – 60

4.1 General introduction to nervous system, neurons, mechanism of propagation of nerve impulse...44 – 45
4.2 Physiology of CNS, PNS, ANS..46 – 48
4.3 Physiology of sensory and motor nervous system....................................49 – 50
4.4 Functions of different parts of brain and physiology of special senses, intelligence, memory, learning and motivation...................51 – 53
4.5 Physiology of sleep and dreams...54 – 55
4.6 EEG..56 – 57
4.7 Physiology of speech and articulation...58 – 59
4.8 Physiology of temperature regulation..60

Table of Contents Page No.

Chapter 5- Physiology of Endocrine glands........................61 – 67

5.1 General introduction to endocrine system..61 – 62
5.2 Classification and characteristics of hormones.....................................63 – 64
5.3 Physiology of all endocrine glands, their functions and their effects..............65 – 67

Chapter 6- Haemopoietic system.......................................68 – 83

6.1 Composition, functions of blood and blood cells, Haemopoiesis (stages and development of RBCs, and WBCs and platelets),..68 – 70
6.2 Composition and functions of bone marrow..71
6.3 Structure, types and functions of haemoglobin.....................................72 – 73
6.4 Mechanism of blood clotting..74 – 75
6.5 Anticoagulants...76 – 78
6.6 Physiological basis of blood groups, plasma proteins...............................79 – 81
6.7 Introduction to anaemia and jaundice...82 – 83

Chapter 7-Immunity...84 – 89

7.1 Classification of immunity: Innate, acquired and artificial........................84 – 85
7.2 Different mechanisms involved in immunity: Humoral (B-cell mediated) and T-Cell mediated immunity.........................86 – 87
7.3 Hypersensitivity...88 – 89

Chapter 8-Physiology of Cardio – Vascular System.............90 - 104

8.1 Functional anatomy of cardiovascular system..90 – 91
8.2 Cardiac cycle..92 – 93
8.3 Heart sound..94 – 95
8.4 Regulation of cardiac output and venous return.....................................96 – 97
8.5 Physiological basis of ECG...98 – 99
8.6 Heart-rate and its regulation & arterial pulse.....................................100 – 102
8.7 Systemic arterial blood pressure and its control...................................103 – 104

Chapter 9- Muscle Physiology..................................105 - 108

9.1 Comparison of physiology of skeletal muscles, Cardiac muscles and smooth muscles...105 – 106
9.2 Physiology of muscle contraction...107 – 108

Table of Contents Page No.

Chapter 10 - Adipose Tissue...109 - 112

10.1 Lipoproteins - VLDL, LDL and HDL triglycerides..............................109 – 110
10.2 Functions of skin, sweat glands and sebaceous glands..........................111 – 112

Chapter 11 - Physiology of male and female reproductive.......113 - 120

11.1 Description of Ovulation..113 – 114
11.2 Spermatogenesis..115 – 116
11.3 Oogenesis...117 - 118
11.4 Menstrual Cycle...119 - 120

Chapter 12 - Physiology of Excretion..............................121 - 129

12.1 Functional anatomy of urinary tract..121 – 122
12.2 Functions of kidney...123 – 124
12.3 Mechanism of formation of urine control of micturition.........................125 – 127
12.4 Formation of faeces and mechanism of defecation...............................128 – 129

Chapter 13 - Special Senses, Sleep and Dreams..................130 - 142

13.1 Physiology of special senses. physiology of sleep and dreams.................130 – 142

Multiple Choice Questions...143 - 169

Chapter - 1

(1.1) Mechanisms of Maintenance of Homeostasis

Homeostasis is a fundamental concept in biology, referring to the ability of living organisms to maintain stable internal conditions despite external changes. This state of equilibrium is crucial for optimal functioning and survival. Here's a detailed exploration of its definition and mechanisms.

Definition of Homeostasis

Homeostasis is defined as the process by which biological systems regulate their internal environment to maintain a stable, constant condition. This includes regulating various parameters such as temperature, pH, electrolyte balance, and glucose levels within specific ranges despite fluctuations in the external environment or internal demands.

Mechanisms of Homeostasis

The maintenance of homeostasis involves several interdependent components that work together in a feedback loop. The primary mechanisms include:

1. Components of Homeostatic Control

Receptor : This component senses changes in the environment (stimuli) and monitors the variable being regulated. For instance, thermoreceptors detect temperature changes.

Control Centre : Often located in the brain, this centre processes information received from receptors and determines the appropriate response. It sets the "normal" range for the variable.

Effector : This component acts on signals from the control centre to bring about a change. Effectors can be muscles or glands that perform functions to restore balance, such as sweating to cool down or shivering to generate heat.

2. Feedback Mechanisms

Homeostatic regulation primarily utilizes two types of feedback mechanisms:

Negative Feedback : This is the most common mechanism where a change in a variable triggers a response that counteracts the initial change, helping to return the system to its set point. For example, if body temperature rises, mechanisms such as sweating are activated to cool the body down.

Positive Feedback : Less common than negative feedback, this mechanism amplifies changes rather than counteracting them. An example is during childbirth, where contractions increase in intensity until delivery occurs.

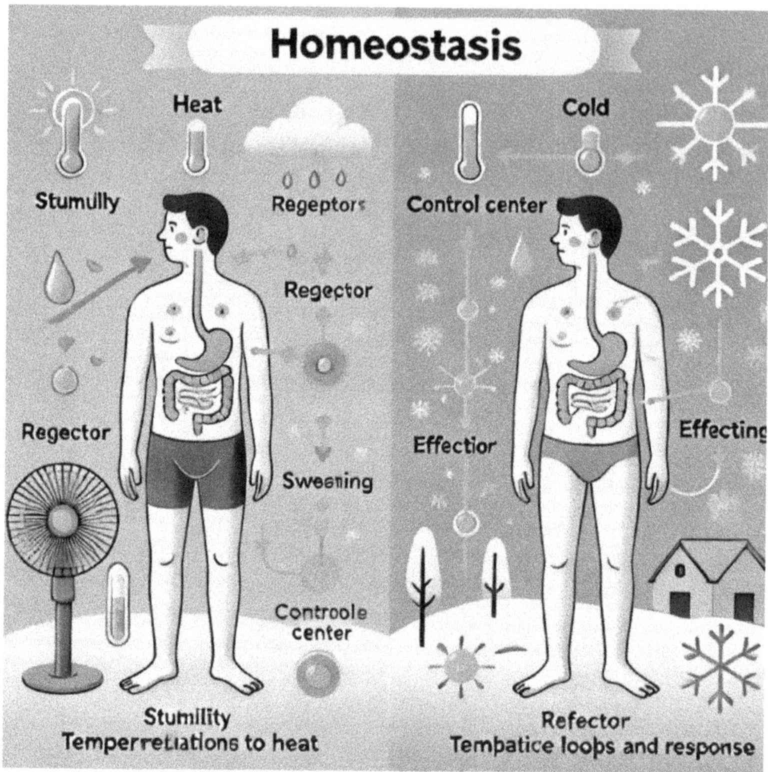

3. Examples of Homeostatic Processes

Thermoregulation : The body maintains its temperature around 37°C (98.6°F) through mechanisms like sweating and shivering.

Blood Glucose Regulation : Insulin and glucagon work to keep blood sugar levels within a narrow range, responding to food intake and energy needs.

Acid-Base Balance : The body regulates pH levels through respiratory and renal adjustments to maintain homeostasis in bodily fluids.

The Contribution of Various Body Systems to Maintaining Homeostasis

Homeostasis is a vital process through which the body maintains stable internal conditions despite external changes. Various organ systems work collaboratively to regulate physiological parameters, ensuring that the body functions optimally. Here's an overview of the roles played by different systems in maintaining homeostasis.

1. Nervous System

Role: The nervous system acts as a control centre, receiving sensory information and coordinating responses.

Mechanism: It uses electrical signals to communicate rapidly between different parts of the body. For instance, thermoreceptors detect changes in temperature, and the hypothalamus processes this information to initiate responses such as sweating or shivering to regulate body temperature.

2. Endocrine System

Role: The endocrine system releases hormones that regulate various bodily functions over longer periods.

Mechanism: Hormones such as insulin and glucagon help maintain blood glucose levels, while others regulate metabolism, growth, and stress responses. The endocrine system interacts with the nervous system to fine-tune homeostatic responses.

3. Cardiovascular System

Role: This system transports nutrients, gases, hormones, and waste products throughout the body.

Mechanism: It helps regulate blood pressure and blood flow to ensure adequate oxygen and nutrient delivery while removing waste. Baroreceptors in blood vessels monitor pressure changes and send signals to the brain to adjust heart rate and vessel diameter accordingly.

4. Respiratory System

Role: The respiratory system regulates gas exchange, primarily oxygen and carbon dioxide levels in the blood.

Mechanism: Chemosensors detect changes in blood gas levels (e.g., increased carbon dioxide) and signal the respiratory centres in the brain to alter breathing rate and depth, thereby maintaining optimal gas concentrations.

5. Urinary System

Role: This system plays a crucial role in regulating water balance, electrolyte levels, and waste removal.

Mechanism: The kidneys filter blood to remove excess substances and waste products while adjusting urine concentration based on hydration status. For example, when water levels are low, the kidneys conserve water by producing concentrated urine.

6. Integumentary System

Role: The skin helps regulate temperature and protects underlying tissues.

Mechanism: It responds to temperature changes through mechanisms such as sweating (cooling) or vasoconstriction (retaining heat). Cutaneous receptors detect temperature variations and relay this information to the nervous system for appropriate responses.

7. Musculoskeletal System

Role: This system supports movement and posture while also contributing to thermoregulation.

Mechanism: Muscle contractions generate heat during physical activity, which can help maintain body temperature. Additionally, muscle metabolism is regulated by hormones that influence energy production.

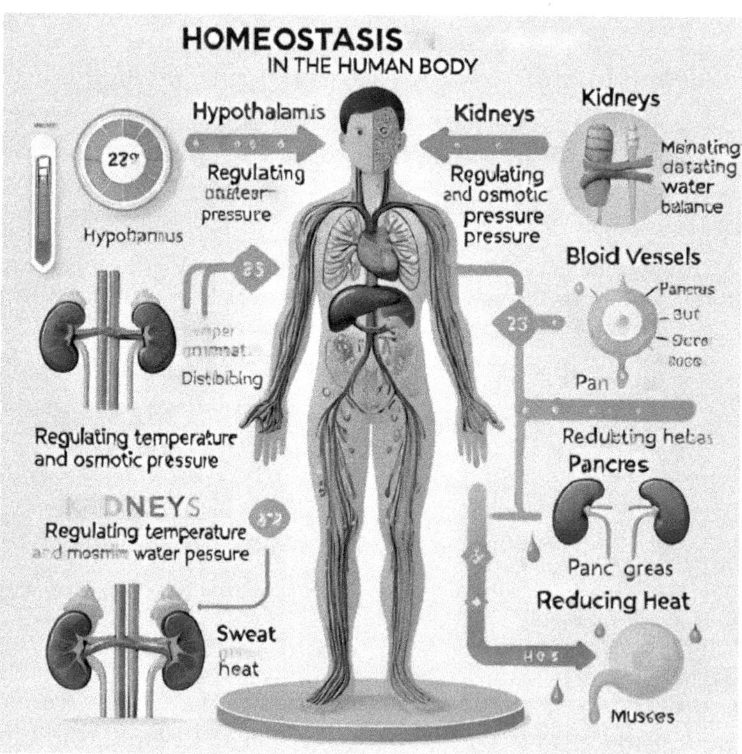

(1.2) Cell physiology

Cell physiology is the study of the biological processes that occur within cells to sustain life. It encompasses various functions and mechanisms that enable cells to maintain homeostasis, grow, reproduce, and respond to their environment. Here's a detailed overview of key aspects of cell physiology based on the search results.

Definition of Cell Physiology

Cell physiology refers to the normal functions and activities of cells, including how they interact with their environment and perform essential life processes. This field examines both animal and plant cells, highlighting similarities in their functions despite structural differences.

Key Functions of Cells

1. Metabolism: Cells metabolize nutrients to produce energy necessary for various cellular activities. This includes catabolic reactions (breaking down molecules) and anabolic reactions (building up molecules).

2. Homeostasis: Cells maintain stable internal conditions through selective permeability of the cell membrane, which regulates the movement of ions and molecules in and out of the cell. This helps control osmotic pressure, pH levels, and ionic composition.

3. Growth and Reproduction: Cells grow by taking in nutrients and expanding in size. They reproduce through processes such as mitosis (for somatic cells) or meiosis (for gametes), ensuring genetic continuity.

4. Communication: Cells communicate with each other through signalling molecules that bind to receptors on their membranes. This intercellular communication is crucial for coordinating physiological responses, such as hormone release and nerve transmission.

5. Transport Mechanisms:
- Passive Transport: Small molecules like oxygen and carbon dioxide move across the cell membrane along concentration gradients without energy expenditure.
- Active Transport: Larger molecules or ions are transported against their concentration gradient using energy (ATP).

6. Structural Support: The cytoskeleton provides shape and structural integrity to the cell, anchoring organelles in place and facilitating movement within the cell.

Cell Organelles and Their Functions

Here is a detailed explanation of cell organelles and their functions:

Organelle	Function	Found In
Nucleus	Controls cellular activities, stores DNA, and regulates gene expression.	Eukaryotic cells (plant and animal).
Mitochondria	Generates ATP through cellular respiration ("powerhouse of the cell").	Eukaryotic cells.
Rough ER	Synthesizes and transports proteins with attached ribosomes.	Eukaryotic cells.
Smooth ER	Synthesizes lipids, detoxifies chemicals, and stores calcium.	Eukaryotic cells.
Ribosomes	Synthesizes proteins by translating mRNA.	Both prokaryotic and eukaryotic cells.
Golgi Apparatus	Modifies, sorts, and packages proteins and lipids for transport.	Eukaryotic cells.
Lysosomes	Breaks down waste, debris, and pathogens with digestive enzymes.	Animal cells (rare in plant cells).
Peroxisomes	Breaks down fatty acids and detoxifies harmful substances.	Eukaryotic cells.
Vacuoles	Stores nutrients, water, and waste; maintains turgor pressure in plants.	Large in plants, smaller in animals.
Chloroplasts	Conducts photosynthesis to produce glucose.	Plant cells and some algae.
Cell Membrane	Regulates the entry and exit of substances, acts as a selective barrier.	Both prokaryotic and eukaryotic cells.
Cell Wall	Provides structural support and protection; maintains shape.	Plant cells, fungi, some prokaryotes.

Organelle	Function	Found In
Cytoplasm	Suspends organelles; site for metabolic activities.	Both prokaryotic and eukaryotic cells.
Cytoskeleton	Provides structure, shape, and aids in movement and transport.	Both prokaryotic and eukaryotic cells.
Centrioles	Organizes microtubules during cell division.	Animal cells.
Cilia and Flagella	Aid in cell movement and help move substances across the cell surface.	Certain prokaryotic and eukaryotic cells.

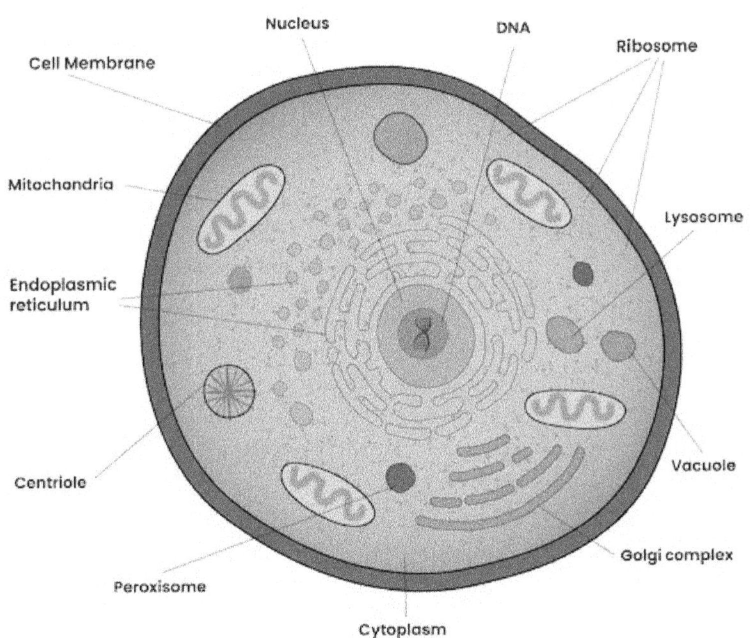

(1.3) Membrane physiology

Membrane physiology is a critical area of study that focuses on the structure and function of cell membranes, which serve as barriers and regulators for cellular environments. Here's an overview based on the search results:

Overview of Cell Membrane Physiology

Structure of the Cell Membrane

- The cell membrane, also known as the plasma membrane, is primarily composed of a phospholipid bilayer. Each phospholipid molecule has a hydrophilic (water-attracting) "head" and two hydrophobic (water-repelling) fatty acid "tails." This arrangement creates a semi-permeable barrier that separates the interior of the cell from the external environment.

- Cholesterol is interspersed within the phospholipid bilayer, contributing to membrane fluidity and stability. It prevents excessive fluidity at high temperatures and maintains flexibility at lower temperatures by interfering with fatty acid interactions.

Functions of the Cell Membrane

1. Selective Permeability: The membrane regulates the entry and exit of substances, allowing small, nonpolar molecules (like oxygen and carbon dioxide) to pass through easily via simple diffusion. In contrast, larger or polar molecules require specific transport mechanisms.

2. Transport Mechanisms:

- Passive Transport: Includes processes like diffusion and facilitated diffusion, where substances move across the membrane without energy expenditure.
- Active Transport: Involves energy (ATP) to move substances against their concentration gradient, using protein pumps.

3. Communication: The cell membrane contains various proteins that act as receptors for signalling molecules, allowing cells to communicate and respond to their environment.

4. Structural Support: The membrane provides structural integrity to the cell while allowing for flexibility and movement. The cytoskeleton interacts with the membrane to maintain cell shape.

Membrane Proteins

- Membrane proteins can be classified into two categories:
  - Integral Proteins: Embedded within the lipid bilayer; they often function as channels or transporters.
  - Peripheral Proteins: Located on the surface of the membrane; they play roles in signalling and maintaining the cell's shape.

Fluid Mosaic Model

- This model describes the cell membrane as a dynamic structure where lipids and proteins can move laterally within the layer, contributing to its fluidity. The presence of cholesterol and various proteins creates a "mosaic" appearance that is essential for various cellular functions.

Explained above information in tabular form:-

Aspect	Description
Structure	Composed of a phospholipid bilayer with embedded proteins, cholesterol, and carbohydrates.
Phospholipid Bilayer	Hydrophilic heads face outward, hydrophobic tails face inward, forming a selective barrier.
Proteins	Integral and peripheral proteins facilitate transport, signalling, and structural support.
Cholesterol	Maintains fluidity and stability of the membrane.
Carbohydrates	Glycoproteins and glycolipids aid in cell recognition and communication.

- **Functions**

Selective Permeability	Regulates the entry and exit of substances.
Passive Transport	Includes diffusion, osmosis, and facilitated diffusion (no energy required).
Active Transport	Moves molecules against the concentration gradient using ATP (e.g., sodium-potassium pump).
Signal Transduction	Receptors detect external signals and relay messages into the cell.
Cell Communication	Glycoproteins and glycolipids enable cell recognition and interaction.
Endocytosis	Engulfs substances into vesicles for internalization.

Aspect	Description
Exocytosis	Expels substances from the cell via vesicles.

- **Key Processes**

Membrane Potential	Ion pumps and channels maintain voltage across the membrane, enabling nerve impulses and muscle contractions.
Fluid Mosaic Model	The membrane is dynamic, with lipids and proteins moving laterally.
Homeostasis	Maintains internal balance by regulating ion concentrations, water, and nutrients.
Cytoskeleton Interaction	Anchors the membrane, maintaining cell shape and enabling movement.

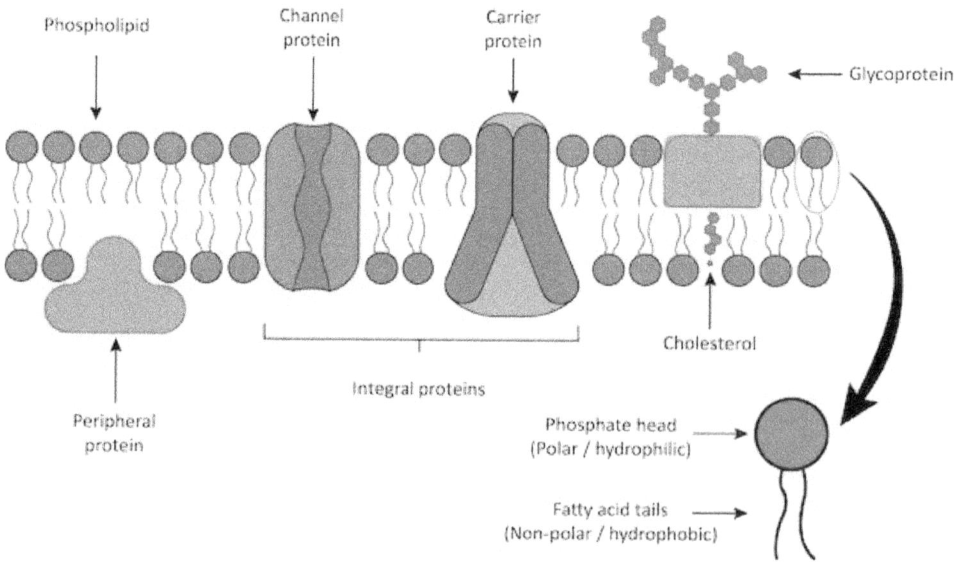

(1.4) Transportation of various substances across cell membrane

The transportation of various substances across the cell membrane is a critical aspect of cell physiology, allowing cells to maintain homeostasis and interact with their environment. This process can be categorized into two main types: passive transport and active transport. Here's a detailed overview based on the search results.

1. Passive Transport –

Passive transport mechanisms do not require energy input from the cell. Instead, they rely on the natural movement of molecules down their concentration gradients.

Types of Passive Transport

Simple Diffusion: This occurs when small, nonpolar molecules (such as oxygen and carbon dioxide) move directly through the lipid bilayer of the cell membrane without assistance. The movement continues until equilibrium is reached across the membrane.

Facilitated Diffusion: Larger or polar molecules, as well as ions, require assistance to cross the membrane. This process involves integral membrane proteins that act as channels or carriers. For example, glucose can enter cells via specific transporter proteins.

Osmosis: A specific type of facilitated diffusion, osmosis refers to the movement of water molecules across a selectively permeable membrane. Water moves in response to solute concentration gradients until equilibrium is achieved.

2. Active Transport –

Active transport mechanisms require energy (usually in the form of ATP) to move substances against their concentration gradients.

Types of Active Transport

Primary Active Transport: This process directly uses ATP to transport molecules against their concentration gradient. A well-known example is the sodium-potassium pump (Na^+/K^+ pump), which maintains high potassium and low sodium concentrations inside the cell by pumping sodium out and potassium in.

Secondary Active Transport: This mechanism uses the energy created by primary active transport to move other substances against their gradients. It often involves symporters or antiporters. For instance, the sodium-glucose symporter (SGLT) utilizes the sodium gradient established by the Na^+/K^+ pump to transport glucose into cells alongside sodium ions.

3. Bulk Transport –

Bulk transport mechanisms involve larger quantities of materials being moved into or out of cells via vesicles.

Types of Bulk Transport

Endocytosis: The process by which cells internalize substances by engulfing them in vesicles. This includes phagocytosis (cell eating) for large particles and pinocytosis (cell drinking) for fluids and small solutes.

Exocytosis: The reverse process where cells expel materials from vesicles into the extracellular environment. This is crucial for processes such as neurotransmitter release in nerve cells.

Amazing Fact -

"The human body contains around 37.2 trillion cells, and each one of these cells is constantly working to keep us alive and healthy".

(1.5) Resting membrane potential and action potential

Resting Membrane Potential (RMP) and Action Potential (AP) are fundamental concepts in cell physiology, particularly in the functioning of excitable cells such as neurons and muscle cells.

Resting Membrane Potential (RMP)

Definition

The resting membrane potential is the electrical potential difference across the plasma membrane of a cell when it is not actively transmitting signals or undergoing significant electrical activity. Typically, this potential is around -70 mV (millivolts), indicating that the interior of the cell is negatively charged relative to the outside environment.

Mechanism

1. Ion Distribution: The RMP is primarily established by the uneven distribution of ions across the cell membrane, particularly potassium (K^+), sodium (Na^+), chloride (Cl^-), and calcium (Ca^{2+}). At rest, K^+ ions are more concentrated inside the cell, while Na^+ ions are more concentrated outside.

2. Selective Permeability: The cell membrane is more permeable to K^+ than to Na^+ due to the presence of specific ion channels. As K^+ ions diffuse out of the cell down their concentration gradient, they leave behind negatively charged proteins and other anions, contributing to the negative charge inside the cell.

3. Sodium-Potassium Pump: This active transport mechanism uses ATP to pump 3 Na^+ ions out of the cell and 2 K^+ ions into the cell, helping maintain the concentration gradients essential for RMP.

Importance

The RMP is crucial for maintaining homeostasis within cells and providing a baseline from which action potentials can be generated. It allows cells to respond quickly to stimuli by changing their membrane potential.

Action Potential (AP)

Definition

An action potential is a rapid, temporary change in the membrane potential that occurs when a neuron or muscle cell is stimulated. This change allows for the transmission of electrical signals along neurons and muscle contraction.

Phases of Action Potential

1. Depolarization: When a stimulus reaches a threshold level, voltage-gated Na^+ channels open, allowing Na^+ ions to rush into the cell. This influx causes depolarization, making the inside of the cell more positive.

2. Repolarization: After reaching a peak positive voltage, Na^+ channels close and voltage-gated K^+ channels open. K^+ ions exit the cell, restoring the negative internal environment.

3. Hyperpolarization: The outflow of K^+ may temporarily overshoot resting levels, leading to hyperpolarization before returning to RMP due to the closing of K^+ channels and action of the sodium-potassium pump.

Propagation

Once initiated, action potentials propagate along the axon without diminishing in strength due to saltatory conduction in myelinated neurons, where APs jump between nodes of Ranvier.

Importance

Action potentials are essential for communication within the nervous system and between nerves and muscles. They enable rapid signalling over long distances, facilitating reflexes and coordinated movements.

(1.6) Acid -base balance, water and electrolyte balance

Acid-base balance and water and electrolyte balance are essential physiological processes that maintain the stability of the internal environment of the body. Here's an overview based on the provided search results.

Acid-Base Balance

Definition

Acid-base balance refers to the mechanisms that maintain the pH of the body's fluids within a narrow range, typically around 7.35 to 7.45 for blood. Deviations from this range can lead to serious health issues, including acidaemia (pH < 7.35) and alkalemia (pH > 7.45) .

Mechanisms of Regulation

1. Chemical Buffers: The first line of defence against pH changes consists of buffer systems in the extracellular fluid (ECF). Key buffer systems include:

- Bicarbonate Buffer System: The most significant buffer in the ECF, it helps maintain pH by balancing carbonic acid (H_2CO_3) and bicarbonate (HCO_3^-) levels.
- Phosphate Buffer System: Important in intracellular fluid and renal function.
- Protein Buffer System: Proteins can act as buffers by binding or releasing hydrogen ions (H^+).

2. Respiratory Regulation: The respiratory system adjusts blood pH by controlling carbon dioxide (CO_2) levels through changes in breathing rate and depth. Increased CO_2 leads to more carbonic acid formation, lowering pH, while decreased CO_2 raises pH .

3. Renal Regulation: The kidneys play a crucial role in long-term acid-base balance by excreting hydrogen ions and reabsorbing bicarbonate. This process is slower than respiratory regulation but is more powerful and can correct significant imbalances over hours to days .

Importance

Maintaining acid-base balance is vital for normal cellular function, enzyme activity, and overall metabolic processes. Disturbances can lead to severe clinical consequences affecting multiple organ systems .

Water and Electrolyte Balance

Definition

Water and electrolyte balance refers to the regulation of fluid volume and composition in the body, ensuring that cells function optimally.

Mechanisms of Regulation

1. Fluid Intake and Output: The body maintains water balance through mechanisms that regulate thirst (driven by osmotic pressure changes) and urine output (controlled by hormones such as antidiuretic hormone or ADH) .

2. Electrolyte Regulation: Electrolytes such as sodium (Na^+), potassium (K^+), calcium (Ca^{2+}), and chloride (Cl^-) are crucial for various physiological functions, including nerve conduction, muscle contraction, and hydration status.
   - The kidneys play a central role in regulating electrolyte levels by filtering blood and adjusting the excretion or reabsorption of these ions based on the body's needs.

3. Hormonal Control: Hormones like aldosterone (which promotes sodium retention) and atrial natriuretic peptide (which promotes sodium excretion) help regulate electrolyte balance.

Importance

Proper water and electrolyte balance is essential for maintaining blood pressure, cellular function, and overall homeostasis. Imbalances can lead to conditions such as dehydration, oedema, or electrolyte disorders, which can significantly impact health.

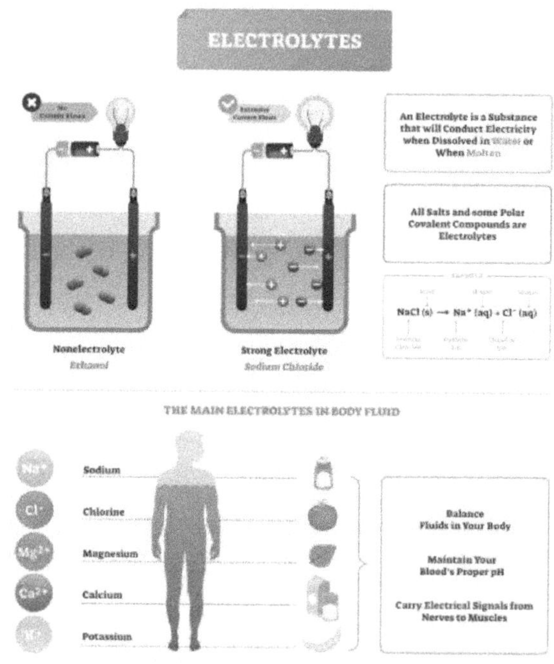

(1.7) Basic components of food

The study of the basic components of food is essential for understanding nutrition and maintaining a healthy diet. Food is composed of various substances known as nutrients, each playing a vital role in the body's functioning. Here's a detailed overview based on the search results:

Components of Food

1. **Carbohydrates**

- Function: Carbohydrates are the primary source of energy for the body. They provide quick energy and are crucial for the functioning of the brain and muscles.
- Types: They can be classified into simple carbohydrates (sugars) and complex carbohydrates (starches).
- Sources: Common sources include bread, rice, potatoes, fruits, and honey.

2. **Fats**

- Function: Fats provide a concentrated source of energy, more than double that of carbohydrates. They are also essential for absorbing fat-soluble vitamins (A, D, E, K) and protecting vital organs.
- Types: Fats can be saturated or unsaturated, with unsaturated fats being healthier options.
- Sources: Found in oils, butter, nuts, dairy products, and fatty meats.

3. **Proteins**

- Function: Proteins are vital for growth, repair of tissues, and overall body maintenance. They serve as building blocks for muscles, skin, enzymes, and hormones.
- Sources: Proteins can be obtained from both animal sources (meat, fish, eggs) and plant sources (beans, lentils, nuts).

4. **Vitamins**

- Function: Vitamins play critical roles in various biochemical processes and help protect against diseases. They are necessary for immune function, energy production, and blood clotting.
- Sources: Different vitamins are found in fruits (vitamin C), vegetables (vitamin A), dairy products (vitamin D), and whole grains.

5. **Minerals**

- Function: Minerals are inorganic elements that support processes such as bone formation, fluid balance, and nerve transmission.
- Sources: Important minerals include calcium (dairy products), iron (red meat), potassium (bananas), and sodium (table salt).

6. Water

- Function: Water is essential for life; it aids in digestion, nutrient transport, temperature regulation, and waste elimination.
- Sources: Water can be obtained from beverages as well as from foods like fruits and vegetables.

7. Fiber (Roughage)

- Function: Fiber aids in digestion by promoting regular bowel movements and preventing constipation. It also helps control blood sugar levels and lowers cholesterol.
- Sources: High-fiber foods include whole grains, fruits, vegetables, legumes, and nuts.

Importance of a Balanced Diet

A balanced diet includes all these components in appropriate proportions to ensure adequate nutrition. A deficiency in any nutrient can lead to health issues such as malnutrition or diseases related to specific vitamin or mineral deficiencies.

(TIP POINT) -

Here is a table that presents the normal vital signs for a healthy adult:

Vital Sign	Normal Range	Unit of Measurement
Heart Rate (Pulse)	60 - 100 beats per minute (bpm)	beats per minute (bpm)
Blood Pressure	Systolic: 90 - 120 mmHg Diastolic: 60 - 80 mmHg	millimetres of mercury (mmHg)
Respiratory Rate	12 - 20 breaths per minute	breaths per minute (bpm)
Body Temperature	97.8 - 99.1°F (36.5 - 37.3°C)	Fahrenheit (°F) / Celsius (°C)
Oxygen Saturation (SpO_2)	95% - 100%	percentage (%)
Blood Glucose	70 - 99 mg/dL (fasting)	milligrams per decilitre (mg/dL)

Chapter – 2

(2.1) Functional anatomy of respiratory system

The functional anatomy of the respiratory system encompasses the structures and mechanisms involved in the process of breathing and gas exchange. Here's a detailed overview based on the search results.

Overview of the Respiratory System

The respiratory system consists of various organs and structures that facilitate the exchange of gases (oxygen and carbon dioxide) between the body and the environment. It can be divided into two main parts: the upper respiratory tract and the lower respiratory tract.

Upper Respiratory Tract

- Nose : The primary entry point for air, equipped with mucous membranes that trap dust and pathogens. Cilia help move trapped particles out.

- Nasal Cavity : Warms, humidifies, and filters incoming air; contains olfactory receptors for smell.

- Sinuses : Air-filled spaces that lighten the skull and contribute to voice resonance.

- Pharynx : A muscular tube that serves both respiratory and digestive systems, directing air to the larynx and food to the oesophagus.

- Larynx : Contains vocal cords; crucial for phonation and protects the trachea against food aspiration.

Lower Respiratory Tract

- Trachea : The windpipe that conducts air to the lungs; reinforced with cartilage rings to prevent collapse.

- Bronchi : The trachea divides into two main bronchi (left and right), which branch into smaller bronchioles within each lung.

- Bronchioles : Small airways that lead to alveoli; they regulate airflow through smooth muscle contraction.

- Alveoli : Tiny, grape-like sacs where gas exchange occurs. They are surrounded by capillaries, allowing oxygen to diffuse into the blood while carbon dioxide diffuses out.

Functional Components

Gas Exchange

The primary function of the respiratory system is gas exchange, which occurs in the alveoli:
- Oxygen from inhaled air diffuses through the alveolar walls into the bloodstream.
- Carbon dioxide from the blood diffuses into the alveoli to be exhaled.

Ventilation

Ventilation involves the movement of air in and out of the lungs:
- Inhalation : Initiated by diaphragm contraction and expansion of intercostal muscles, increasing thoracic volume and decreasing pressure within the thoracic cavity, allowing air to flow in.
- Exhalation : Generally a passive process where elastic recoil of lung tissue expels air. Active exhalation may involve abdominal muscles during vigorous activities.

Regulation of Breathing

Breathing is regulated by:
- The autonomic nervous system, particularly centres in the medulla oblongata and pons, which control rhythm and depth based on carbon dioxide levels in blood.
- Chemoreceptors detect changes in blood pH, carbon dioxide, and oxygen levels, adjusting ventilation accordingly.

Additional Functions

The respiratory system also plays several other roles:
- Filtration : Mucus traps particles; cilia move mucus out of the respiratory tract.
- Humidification : Moistens incoming air to protect lung tissues.
- Temperature Regulation : Warms inhaled air to body temperature.
- Acid-Base Balance : Helps maintain pH balance by regulating carbon dioxide levels through ventilation.

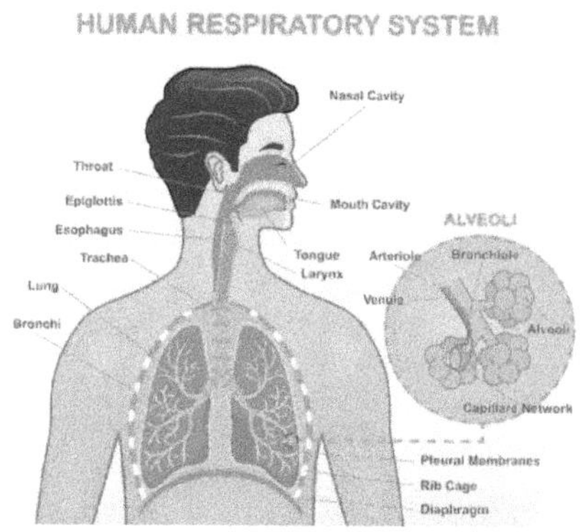

(2.2) Ventilation, Mechanism of respiration, Exchange and transport of gases, Neural and chemical control of respiration, Artificial respiration, Asphyxia, Hypoxia

Definition of Ventilation

Ventilation refers to the physical process of moving air in and out of the lungs, facilitating gas exchange with the environment. It involves inhalation (taking air into the lungs) and exhalation (expelling air from the lungs) and is essential for maintaining adequate oxygen levels and removing carbon dioxide from the body.

Mechanism of Respiration

Respiration encompasses two main processes: External respiration and Internal respiration.

1. External Respiration : This process occurs in the lungs, where oxygen from inhaled air diffuses across the alveolar membrane into the blood, while carbon dioxide diffuses from the blood into the alveoli to be exhaled. The respiratory membrane, composed of alveolar walls and capillary walls, facilitates this gas exchange.

2. Internal Respiration : This involves the exchange of gases at the cellular level, where oxygen is delivered to tissues and carbon dioxide is collected as a waste product. Oxygen is utilized in cellular metabolism, while carbon dioxide produced is transported back to the lungs for removal.

Exchange and Transport of Gases

- Gas Exchange : Takes place in the alveoli where oxygen enters the bloodstream, and carbon dioxide is expelled. The efficiency of gas exchange depends on factors such as surface area, diffusion distance, and partial pressure gradients of gases.

- Transport of Gases : Oxygen is primarily transported in the blood bound to haemoglobin within red blood cells, while carbon dioxide is transported in three forms: dissolved in plasma, as bicarbonate ions (HCO_3^-), and bound to haemoglobin. The conversion of carbon dioxide to bicarbonate occurs in red blood cells, helping to regulate blood pH.

Neural and Chemical Control of Respiration

- Neural Control : The respiratory centres located in the brainstem (medulla oblongata and pons) regulate the rhythm and depth of breathing. These centres receive input from chemoreceptors that monitor levels of carbon dioxide, oxygen, and pH in the blood.

- Chemical Control : Chemoreceptors respond to changes in blood chemistry:
  - Central Chemoreceptors : Located in the medulla, they primarily respond to changes in carbon dioxide levels.
  - Peripheral Chemoreceptors : Located in carotid and aortic bodies, they detect low oxygen levels and high carbon dioxide levels, stimulating increased ventilation when necessary.

Artificial Respiration

Artificial respiration refers to techniques used to assist or replace spontaneous breathing when an individual cannot breathe adequately on their own. Common methods include:
- Positive Pressure Ventilation : Using mechanical ventilators to push air into the lungs.
- Bag-Valve-Mask (BVM) Ventilation : A manual method where a bag is squeezed to force air into a patient's lungs through a mask.

These techniques are critical in emergency medicine and critical care settings.

Asphyxia

Asphyxia is a condition resulting from insufficient oxygen reaching the tissues due to various causes such as choking, drowning, or suffocation. It leads to hypoxia (lack of oxygen) and can result in unconsciousness or death if not promptly addressed. Symptoms may include cyanosis (bluish skin), confusion, and respiratory distress.

Hypoxia

Hypoxia refers specifically to a deficiency of oxygen in tissues. It can be caused by various factors including:
- Low atmospheric oxygen levels (high altitudes).
- Respiratory diseases (e.g., COPD, pneumonia).
- Anaemia or carbon monoxide poisoning.

Hypoxia can lead to cellular dysfunction and organ failure if not corrected quickly.

(2.3) Introduction to Pulmonary Function Tests

Pulmonary function tests (PFTs) are essential diagnostic tools used to evaluate the respiratory function of patients. They help in assessing lung health, diagnosing respiratory conditions, and monitoring the effectiveness of treatments. Here's an introduction to pulmonary function tests based on the search results.

Introduction to Pulmonary Function Tests

Pulmonary function tests (PFTs) are non-invasive assessments that measure how well the lungs work. They are crucial for diagnosing and managing various respiratory diseases such as chronic obstructive pulmonary disease (COPD), asthma, and pulmonary fibrosis. PFTs evaluate several aspects of lung function, including airflow, lung volume, and gas exchange capabilities.

Purpose of PFTs

- Diagnosis : PFTs help identify lung diseases by measuring various parameters like forced vital capacity (FVC) and forced expiratory volume in one second (FEV1). These measurements can indicate the presence of obstructive or restrictive lung diseases.
- Monitoring : For patients with known respiratory conditions, PFTs are used to monitor disease progression and response to treatment.
- Preoperative Assessment : PFTs may be performed before surgeries, especially those involving anaesthesia, to evaluate a patient's lung function and potential risks.
- Evaluation of Symptoms : They are often ordered for patients experiencing symptoms like shortness of breath, wheezing, or chronic cough.

Types of Pulmonary Function Tests

1. **Spirometry :** The most common PFT, measuring how much air a person can inhale and exhale, as well as how quickly they can exhale. It helps diagnose conditions like asthma and COPD.

2. **Lung Volume Measurement :** This test assesses the total volume of air in the lungs, including the amount left after exhalation.

3. **Diffusion Capacity Test :** Measures how well oxygen passes from the lungs into the bloodstream by assessing gas exchange efficiency in the alveoli.

4. **Pulse Oximetry :** While not a traditional PFT, this test measures oxygen saturation in the blood and provides quick insights into respiratory function.

5. Exercise Testing : Evaluates how well the lungs perform under physical stress, often using a six-minute walk test to assess oxygen needs during activity.

Interpretation of Results

The results from PFTs must be interpreted in conjunction with patient history, physical examination findings, and other diagnostic tests. Abnormal results can indicate various conditions:

- Obstructive Lung Disease : Characterized by reduced airflow (e.g., asthma, COPD).
- Restrictive Lung Disease : Indicated by reduced lung volumes (e.g., pulmonary fibrosis).
- Diffusion Impairment : Suggests issues with gas exchange efficiency.

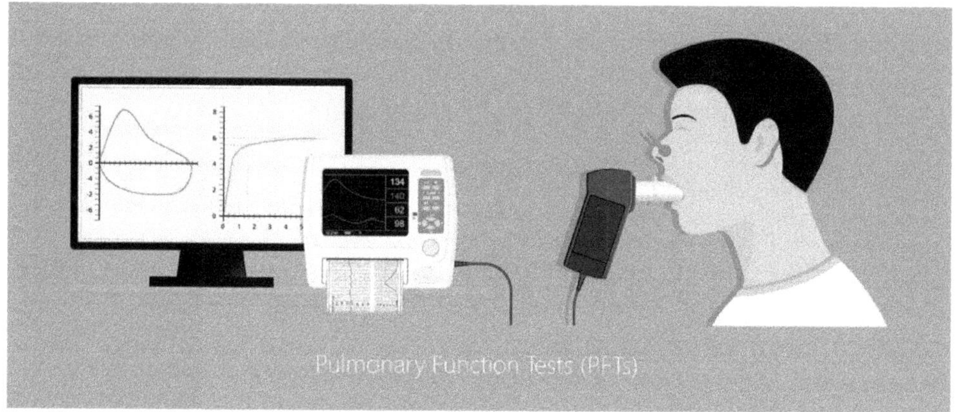

The **normal values** for **Pulmonary Function Tests (PFTs)** vary depending on several factors such as age, gender, height, and ethnicity. PFTs are used to measure the function of the lungs and assess how well they are working. Here are some of the key measurements typically included in PFTs:

1. Forced Vital Capacity (FVC): The total volume of air that can be exhaled forcefully and quickly after taking a deep breath.

2. Forced Expiratory Volume in 1 second (FEV_1): The amount of air exhaled in the first second of a forced exhalation.

3. Peak Expiratory Flow (PEF): The maximum speed at which a person can exhale air.

4. Residual Volume (RV): The volume of air remaining in the lungs after a forceful exhalation.

5. Total Lung Capacity (TLC): The total volume of air in the lungs after a maximum inhalation (sum of all lung volumes).

6. Functional Residual Capacity (FRC): The amount of air remaining in the lungs after a normal exhalation.

7. Inspiratory Reserve Volume (IRV): The additional amount of air that can be inhaled after a normal inhalation.

8. Expiratory Reserve Volume (ERV): The additional amount of air that can be exhaled after a normal exhalation.

9. Diffusing Capacity for Carbon Monoxide (DLCO): Measures how effectively gases (like oxygen) are transferred from the lungs into the bloodstream.

10. Tidal Volume (TV): The amount of air breathed in and out during normal, quiet breathing.

Here is a table with **normal values for common Pulmonary Function Tests (PFTs)**:

Test	Normal Range	Unit of Measurement
Forced Vital Capacity (FVC)	80% - 120% of the predicted value	Liters
Forced Expiratory Volume in 1 second (FEV_1)	80% - 120% of the predicted value	Liters
FEV_1/FVC Ratio	> 0.7 or > 70%	Ratio (percentage)
Peak Expiratory Flow (PEF)	400 - 600 liters per minute (for adults)	Liters per minute
Residual Volume (RV)	1.5 - 2.5 liters	Liters
Total Lung Capacity (TLC)	6 - 7 liters	Liters
Functional Residual Capacity (FRC)	2.5 - 3.5 liters	Liters
Inspiratory Reserve Volume (IRV)	2 - 3 liters	Liters
Expiratory Reserve Volume (ERV)	1 - 1.5 liters	Liters
Diffusing Capacity for Carbon Monoxide (DLCO)	80% - 120% of the predicted value	mL/min/mmHg
Tidal Volume (TV)	500 milliliters	Milliliters

Important Notes:

- **Predicted values** depend on factors like age, sex, height, and ethnicity.
- **FEV_1/FVC ratio** < 0.7 indicates obstructive lung diseases.
- A decreased **FVC** without a reduced **FEV_1/FVC ratio** suggests restrictive lung diseases.

These values represent general guidelines and are used to evaluate the health of the lungs and detect potential pulmonary disorders.

Chapter - 3

(3.1) Functional anatomy of gastro -intestinal tract

The functional anatomy of the gastrointestinal (GI) tract is essential for understanding how the body processes food, absorbs nutrients, and eliminates waste. The GI tract is a complex system composed of various organs and structures that work together to facilitate digestion and absorption. Here's an overview based on the provided search results.

Overview of the Gastrointestinal Tract

The gastrointestinal tract is a continuous tube that extends from the mouth to the anus, consisting of several key organs:

1. **Oral Cavity :** The starting point of digestion, where food is mechanically broken down by teeth and mixed with saliva, which contains enzymes that begin the digestion of carbohydrates and fats.
2. **Pharynx :** A muscular passage that connects the oral cavity to the oesophagus. It plays a role in swallowing by directing food into the oesophagus while preventing it from entering the nasal cavity or trachea.
3. **Oesophagus :** A muscular tube that transports food from the pharynx to the stomach through coordinated contractions known as peristalsis. It has both skeletal and smooth muscle components, facilitating voluntary and involuntary control during swallowing.
4. **Stomach :** A hollow organ that stores food and mixes it with gastric juices, including hydrochloric acid and digestive enzymes. The stomach's muscular walls churn food into a semi-liquid form called chyme, which is then gradually released into the small intestine.
5. **Small Intestine:** Comprising three segments (duodenum, jejunum, ileum), the small intestine is where most digestion and nutrient absorption occur. The duodenum receives chyme from the stomach along with bile from the liver and digestive enzymes from the pancreas, while the jejunum and ileum are primarily responsible for absorbing nutrients into the bloodstream.
6. **Large Intestine :** Also known as the colon, it absorbs water and electrolytes from indigestible food matter, converting it into stool. The large intestine consists of several parts: cecum, ascending colon, transverse colon, descending colon, sigmoid colon, rectum, and anal canal.
7. **Accessory Organs :** These include salivary glands (which produce saliva), liver (which produces bile), gallbladder (which stores bile), and pancreas (which secretes digestive enzymes). These organs play critical roles in digestion but are not part of the GI tract itself.

Histological Layers of the GI Tract

The GI tract is composed of four histological layers from innermost to outermost:

1. Mucosa : This innermost layer consists of epithelial tissue that lines the lumen of the GI tract. It contains specialized cells for secretion (mucus, enzymes) and absorption.

2. Submucosa : A connective tissue layer containing blood vessels, lymphatics, and nerves (including the submucosal plexus) that support the mucosa.

3. Muscularis Externa : Composed of two layers of smooth muscle (inner circular and outer longitudinal) responsible for peristalsis and segmentation movements. The myenteric plexus lies between these muscle layers and regulates motility.

4. Serosa/Adventitia : The outermost layer; serosa covers intraperitoneal organs with a smooth membrane, while adventitia covers retroperitoneal organs, providing structural support.

Functions of the Gastrointestinal Tract

- Digestion : Mechanical and chemical breakdown of food into smaller components.
- Absorption : Nutrients are absorbed primarily in the small intestine.
- Excretion : Waste products are eliminated through defecation.
- Immunological Defence : The acidic environment in the stomach helps destroy pathogens.

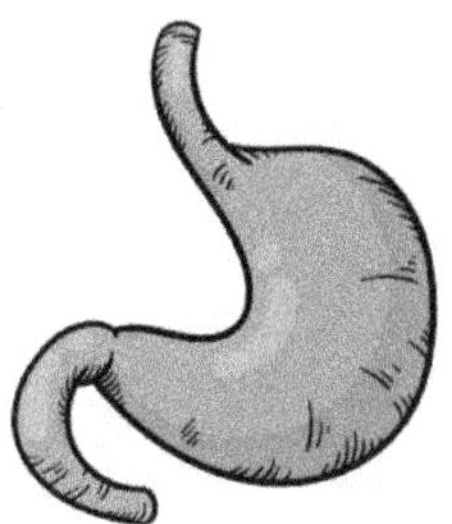

(3.2) Mechanism of secretion and composition of different digestive juices

Mechanism of Secretion and Composition of Different Digestive Juices

The gastrointestinal (GI) tract relies on various digestive juices to break down food, absorb nutrients, and facilitate digestion. These secretions are produced by different organs and are regulated by a complex interplay of neural and hormonal mechanisms. Below is an overview of the mechanisms of secretion and the composition of key digestive juices.

1. Mechanism of Secretion

- **Neural Control :** The secretion of digestive juices is primarily regulated by the autonomic nervous system, particularly through the vagus nerve. The thought, smell, or taste of food can stimulate secretory responses even before food enters the stomach (cephalic phase).

- **Hormonal Control :** Various hormones play critical roles in regulating digestive secretions:

- **Gastrin :** Secreted by G cells in the stomach in response to food presence, particularly proteins. Gastrin stimulates parietal cells to secrete gastric acid (HCl) and promotes gastric motility.

- **Cholecystokinin (CCK) :** Released from I cells in the duodenum in response to fatty acids and amino acids. CCK stimulates the pancreas to release digestive enzymes and the gallbladder to release bile.

- **Secretin :** Produced by S cells in the duodenum in response to acidic chyme. Secretin stimulates the pancreas to secrete bicarbonate, neutralizing gastric acid entering the small intestine.

- **Local Reflexes :** Mechanical and chemical stimuli from food in the GI tract also trigger local reflexes that enhance secretion. For example, distension of the stomach or presence of chyme in the small intestine activates local enteric nervous system pathways.

2. Composition of Digestive Juices

Saliva :

Composition : Contains water, electrolytes (sodium, potassium, chloride), mucus, enzymes (salivary amylase for starch digestion and lingual lipase for fat digestion), and antimicrobial agents (lysozyme).

- **Function :** Initiates digestion and lubricates food for swallowing.

Gastric Juice :

Composition : Primarily consists of hydrochloric acid (HCl), pepsinogen (inactive enzyme that converts to pepsin), intrinsic factor (essential for vitamin B12 absorption), and mucus.

- **Function :** Acidic environment aids protein digestion, activates pepsinogen to pepsin, and provides a barrier against pathogens.

Pancreatic Juice :

Composition : Contains digestive enzymes (amylase for carbohydrates, lipase for fats, proteases like trypsin and chymotrypsin for proteins) and bicarbonate ions.

- **Function :** Neutralizes acidic chyme from the stomach and digests macronutrients in the small intestine.

Bile Juice :

Composition : Composed of bile salts (derived from cholesterol), bilirubin (a breakdown product of haemoglobin), cholesterol, electrolytes, and water.

- **Function :** Emulsifies fats, aiding in their digestion and absorption in the small intestine.

Intestinal Juice :

Composition : Secreted by intestinal glands; contains water, mucus, electrolytes, and various enzymes (e.g., maltase, sucrase).

- **Function :** Completes digestion of carbohydrates and proteins while providing a medium for nutrient absorption.

(3.3) Function of glands and organs with their digestion and absorption

The digestive process involves several organs, each contributing specific functions to ensure the breakdown of food and absorption of nutrients. Here's an overview of the roles of the salivary glands, stomach, liver, pancreas, small intestine, and large intestine in digestion and absorption.

1. Salivary Glands

- **Function :** The salivary glands produce saliva, which initiates the digestive process. Saliva contains enzymes such as amylase that begin the breakdown of carbohydrates into simpler sugars. It also lubricates food, facilitating swallowing and forming a bolus for easier passage through the oesophagus.

- **Composition :** Saliva consists of water, electrolytes (sodium, potassium, bicarbonate), mucins (for lubrication), enzymes (amylase and lipase), and antimicrobial agents (such as lysozyme) that protect the oral cavity from pathogens.

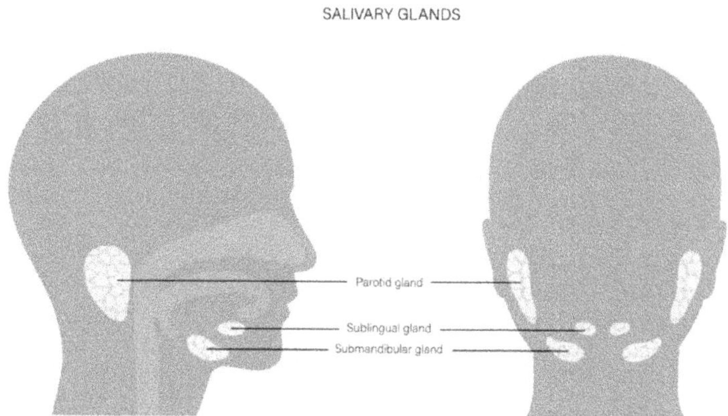

2. Stomach

- **Function :** The stomach serves as a storage site for food and plays a crucial role in digestion. It secretes gastric juices that contain hydrochloric acid (HCl) and pepsinogen (which converts to pepsin), facilitating protein digestion. The acidic environment also helps kill bacteria and activates digestive enzymes.

- **Composition :** Gastric juice is composed of HCl, pepsinogen, intrinsic factor (important for vitamin B12 absorption), and mucus that protects the stomach lining from acidity.

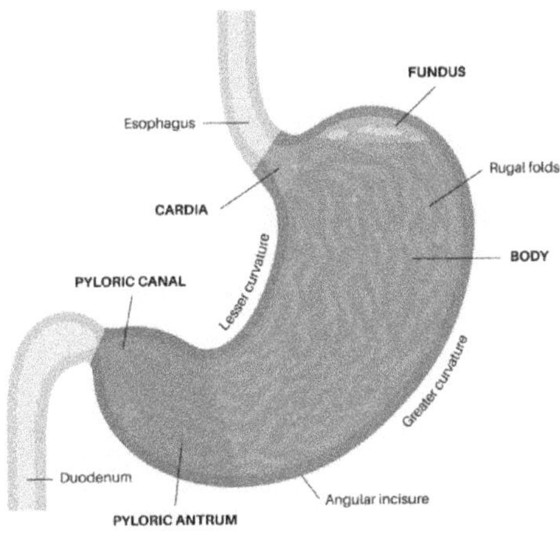

3. Liver

- **Function :** The liver produces bile, which is essential for fat digestion and absorption. Bile emulsifies fats, increasing their surface area for enzymatic action. The liver also processes nutrients absorbed from the small intestine and detoxifies harmful substances.

- **Composition :** Bile contains bile salts (derived from cholesterol), bilirubin (a waste product from red blood cell breakdown), cholesterol, and electrolytes.

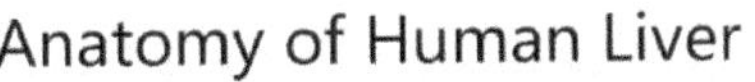

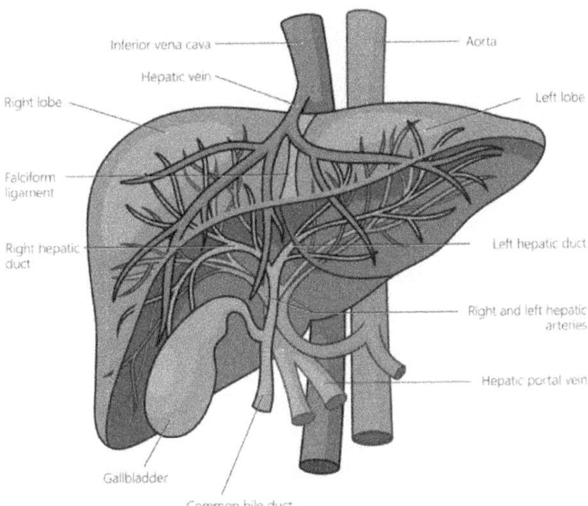

4. Pancreas

- **Function :** The pancreas produces pancreatic juice, which contains digestive enzymes that break down carbohydrates (amylase), proteins (trypsin and chymotrypsin), and fats (lipase). It also secretes bicarbonate to neutralize gastric acid entering the small intestine.

- **Composition :** Pancreatic juice is rich in digestive enzymes and bicarbonate ions, which help create an optimal pH for enzyme activity in the small intestine.

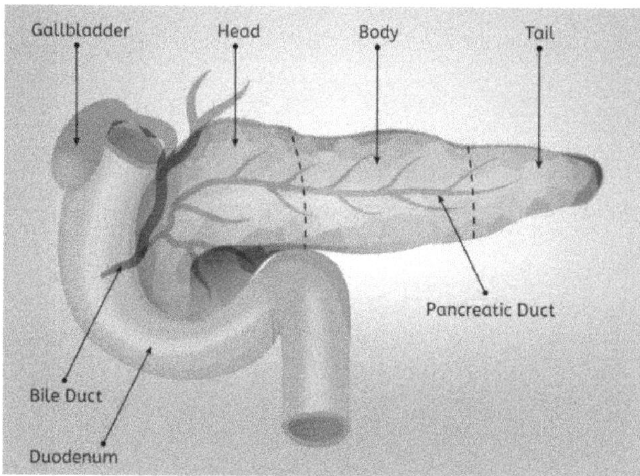

5. Small Intestine

- **Function :** The small intestine is the primary site for digestion and nutrient absorption. It receives chyme from the stomach along with bile and pancreatic juices, facilitating the breakdown of macronutrients into absorbable units (amino acids, fatty acids, monosaccharides).

- **Composition :** The intestinal lining contains villi and microvilli that increase surface area for absorption. Intestinal juice also contains enzymes that further digest carbohydrates and proteins.

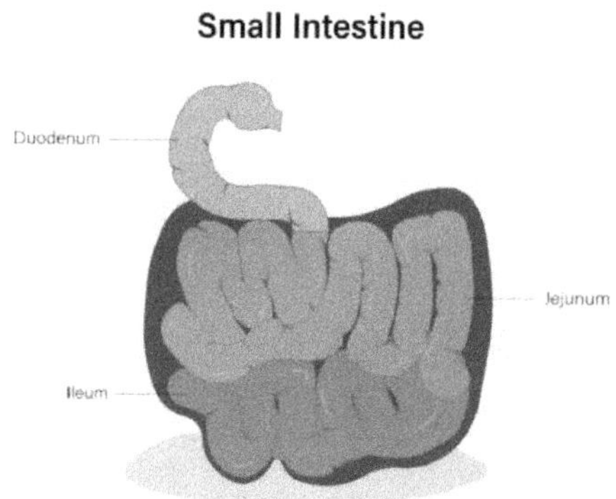

6. Large Intestine

- **Function :** The large intestine primarily absorbs water and electrolytes from indigestible food matter, transforming it into solid waste (faeces). It also houses beneficial bacteria that aid in fermentation of undigested materials.

- Composition : The contents of the large intestine include water, electrolytes, fiber, bacteria, and waste products. Mucus is secreted to facilitate the passage of stool.

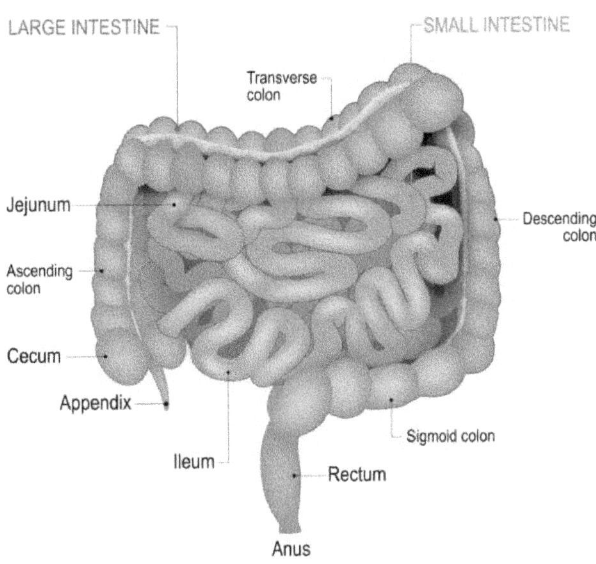

(Amazing Fact) –

" The adult human small intestine, when stretched out, is about **20 feet long**!"

(3.4) Movements of the gut (deglutition, peristalsis, defecation) and their control

Movements of the Gut: Deglutition, Peristalsis, and Defecation

The gastrointestinal (GI) tract is responsible for the digestion and absorption of nutrients, and it relies on several coordinated movements to facilitate these processes. Key movements include deglutition (swallowing), peristalsis, and defecation. Each of these movements is controlled by intricate neural and muscular mechanisms.

1. Deglutition (Swallowing)

- **Definition :** Deglutition is the process of swallowing food or liquid from the mouth into the oesophagus.

- **Phases:**
  - Oral Phase : This voluntary phase involves the tongue pushing the bolus of food to the back of the mouth, triggering the swallowing reflex.
  - Pharyngeal Phase : This involuntary phase begins when the bolus reaches the pharynx. The soft palate elevates to close off the nasal cavity, and the larynx rises to prevent food from entering the trachea. The pharyngeal muscles contract to push the bolus into the oesophagus.
  - Oesophageal Phase : The bolus moves down the oesophagus through peristaltic waves—coordinated contractions of smooth muscle that propel food toward the stomach.

2. Peristalsis

- **Definition :** Peristalsis is a series of wave-like muscle contractions that move food through the digestive tract.

- **Mechanism :**
  - It involves coordinated contractions of circular and longitudinal muscles in the GI tract. When a segment of the gut contracts, it narrows and pushes contents forward, while adjacent segments relax.
  - This process occurs throughout the entire length of the GI tract, from the oesophagus to the intestines, facilitating digestion and absorption by moving food along and mixing it with digestive juices.

3. Defecation

- **Definition :** Defecation is the process of expelling faeces from the rectum through the anus.
- **Mechanism :**
  - The process begins with mass movements in the colon that push faeces into the rectum, stimulating stretch receptors in its walls. This initiates the defecation reflex.
  - As faeces fill the rectum, signals are sent to the brain indicating an urge to defecate. The internal anal sphincter (involuntary control) relaxes while voluntary control over the external anal sphincter allows for conscious decision-making regarding defecation.

- If defecation is appropriate, abdominal muscles contract (often aided by techniques like the Valsalva maneuver), increasing intra-abdominal pressure to help expel faeces. If it is not an appropriate time, one can voluntarily tighten the external anal sphincter to delay defecation.

Control Mechanisms

- Neural Control :

- The autonomic nervous system regulates these movements through reflex arcs involving both central and peripheral pathways.
- For example, stretch receptors in the rectum trigger reflexes that promote peristalsis in both proximal and distal segments of the colon.

- Hormonal Control :

- Hormones such as gastrin and cholecystokinin influence gut motility and secretions that assist in digestion.

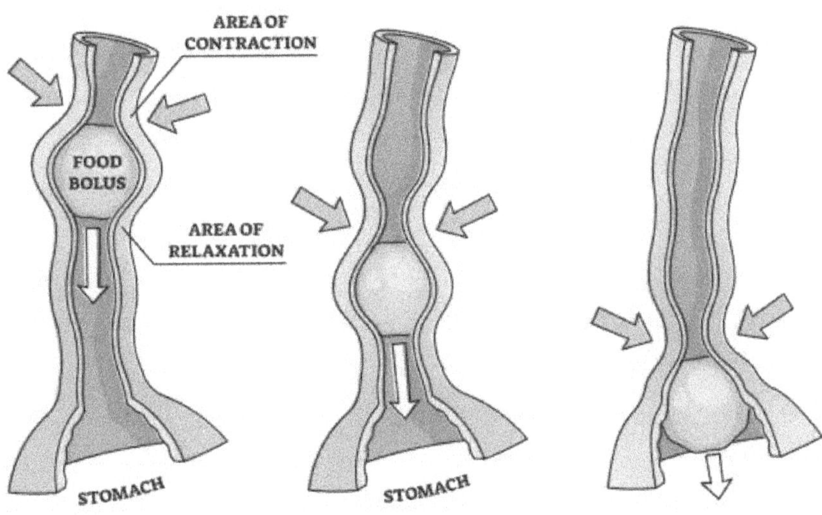

(3.5) Enteric nervous system

The enteric nervous system (ENS) is a complex network of neurons that governs the function of the gastrointestinal tract. Often referred to as the "second brain," the ENS operates independently of the central nervous system (CNS) but maintains communication with it. Here's an overview based on the provided search results.

Definition and Structure

- **Enteric Nervous System (ENS) :** The ENS is a subdivision of the autonomic nervous system, consisting of approximately 200 to 600 million neurons embedded in the walls of the gastrointestinal tract, extending from the oesophagus to the rectum. It includes two major plexuses:

  - Myenteric Plexus : Located between the longitudinal and circular muscle layers, primarily responsible for regulating gut motility.
  - Submucosal Plexus : Situated in the submucosa, it controls local secretions, blood flow, and absorption.

Functions of the Enteric Nervous System

1. Motor Control : The ENS coordinates peristalsis and segmentation movements, facilitating the propulsion and mixing of intestinal contents. This is achieved through intricate reflex arcs that involve sensory neurons detecting changes in gut content and distension.

2. Secretion Regulation : The ENS regulates digestive secretions by controlling mucosal glands and influencing fluid exchange between the gut lumen and surrounding tissues. Secretomotor neurons release neurotransmitters like acetylcholine and vasoactive intestinal peptide (VIP) to modulate secretion.

3. Local Blood Flow : The ENS regulates blood flow to the gastrointestinal tract by influencing vascular smooth muscle, ensuring adequate perfusion during digestion.

4. Sensory Processing : The ENS contains sensory neurons that respond to mechanical and chemical stimuli within the gut. These neurons relay information about gut contents, acidity, and distension, allowing for appropriate motor responses.

5. Immune Function : The ENS interacts with the immune system in the gut, helping to coordinate responses to pathogens and maintain homeostasis. It plays a role in detecting harmful bacteria and initiating protective reflexes like vomiting or diarrhoea.

Neural Control Mechanisms

- The ENS can function autonomously but is also influenced by both sympathetic and parasympathetic inputs from the CNS. It communicates with the CNS primarily via the vagus nerve, forming part of what is known as the gut-brain axis.

- Neurotransmitters such as serotonin, dopamine, and opioids are synthesized within the ENS, contributing to its complex signalling capabilities.

Clinical Significance

- Disorders affecting the ENS can lead to various gastrointestinal issues such as irritable bowel syndrome (IBS), constipation, or diarrhoea.
- There is increasing evidence linking enteric dysfunction with neurological conditions like Parkinson's disease and Alzheimer's disease, highlighting the bidirectional relationship between gut health and brain function.

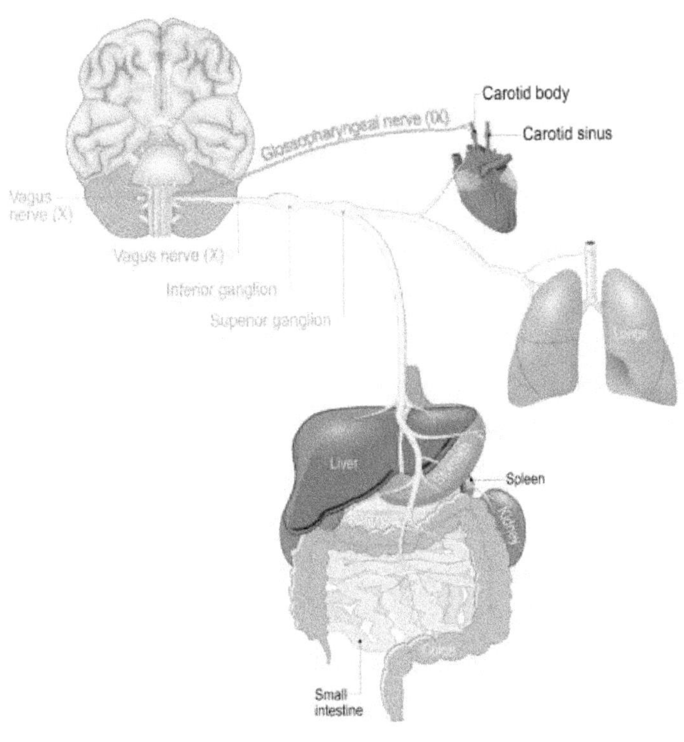

(3.6) Digestion and metabolism of proteins, fats and Carbohydrates

The digestion and metabolism of macronutrients, proteins, fats, and carbohydrates are essential processes that provide energy and building blocks for the body. Each macronutrient undergoes specific digestive processes, leading to absorption and utilization in metabolic pathways.

1. Digestion and Absorption of Proteins

- Digestion :

- Stomach : The digestion of proteins begins in the stomach, where gastric juices containing hydrochloric acid (HCl) and the enzyme pepsin break down proteins into smaller polypeptides. The acidic environment denatures proteins, making them more accessible to enzymatic action.

- Small Intestine : As chyme enters the small intestine, it mixes with pancreatic juices rich in proteolytic enzymes such as trypsin, chymotrypsin, and elastase. These enzymes further break down polypeptides into smaller peptides and amino acids.

- Brush Border Enzymes : The intestinal lining releases additional enzymes (e.g., carboxypeptidase, aminopeptidase) that convert peptides into free amino acids.

- Absorption :

- Amino acids are absorbed through the intestinal wall via sodium-dependent transporters into the bloodstream. They are then transported to the liver and other tissues for protein synthesis and metabolic functions.

2. Digestion and Absorption of Fats

- Digestion :

- Mouth : Lipid digestion begins in the mouth with the action of lingual lipase.
- Stomach : Gastric lipase continues fat digestion in the stomach, but significant fat digestion occurs in the small intestine.
- Small Intestine : Bile salts from the liver emulsify fats, breaking them into smaller droplets to increase surface area for enzymatic action. Pancreatic lipase then hydrolyses triglycerides into free fatty acids and monoglycerides.

- Absorption :

- Fatty acids and monoglycerides are absorbed through the intestinal wall via passive diffusion or through specific transport proteins. Inside intestinal cells, they are reassembled into triglycerides and packaged into chylomicrons for transport via the lymphatic system before entering the bloodstream.

3. Digestion and Absorption of Carbohydrates

- Digestion :

- Mouth : Salivary amylase begins carbohydrate digestion by breaking down starches into maltose and dextrin.
- Small Intestine: Pancreatic amylase continues carbohydrate digestion in the small intestine. Brush border enzymes (e.g., maltase, sucrase, lactase) further break down disaccharides into monosaccharides (glucose, fructose, galactose).

- Absorption :

- Monosaccharides are absorbed through the intestinal wall via sodium-glucose transporters (SGLT) or facilitated diffusion (fructose). They enter the bloodstream and are transported to the liver for further metabolism.

Summary of Key Points

- Proteins are digested primarily in the stomach and small intestine, where they are broken down into amino acids for absorption.

- Fats undergo emulsification by bile salts in the small intestine before being digested by pancreatic lipase; they are absorbed as fatty acids and monoglycerides.

- Carbohydrates begin digestion in the mouth and continue in the small intestine; monosaccharides are absorbed directly into the bloodstream.

(3.7) Vitamins & Minerals

Vitamins and Minerals: Overview

Vitamins and minerals are essential nutrients that play critical roles in various bodily functions, including metabolism, immune function, and bone health. This overview covers the sources, daily requirements, functions, and manifestations of hypo- and hypervitaminosis for key vitamins and minerals.

Vitamins & Minerals: Sources, Daily Requirements, Functions, and Manifestations of Deficiency and Excess

Vitamin	Sources	Daily Requirement	Functions	Deficiency (Hypovitaminosis)	Excess (Hypervitaminosis)
Vitamin A	Liver, carrots, sweet potatoes, spinach, dairy	700-900 µg/day	Vision, immune function, skin health	Night blindness, dry skin, impaired immunity	Nausea, liver damage, birth defects
Vitamin D	Sunlight, fortified milk, fatty fish	600-800 IU/day	Calcium absorption, bone health	Rickets (children), osteomalacia (adults)	Hypercalcemia, kidney damage
Vitamin E	Nuts, seeds, vegetable oils, spinach	15 mg/day	Antioxidant, protects cell membranes	Neuropathy, muscle weakness	Increased bleeding risk
Vitamin K	Leafy greens, broccoli, liver	90-120 µg/day	Blood clotting, bone health	Bleeding disorders	Rare; clotting issues
Vitamin C	Citrus fruits, berries, tomatoes, peppers	75-90 mg/day	Antioxidant, collagen synthesis, immunity	Scurvy (bleeding gums, fatigue)	Gastrointestinal distress

Vitamin	Sources	Daily Requirement	Functions	Deficiency (Hypovitaminosis)	Excess (Hypervitaminosis)
Vitamin B1 (Thiamine)	Whole grains, pork, legumes	1.1-1.2 mg/day	Energy metabolism, nerve function	Beriberi (weakness, heart failure), Wernicke's encephalopathy	Rare; possible irritability
Vitamin B2 (Riboflavin)	Dairy, eggs, green vegetables	1.1-1.3 mg/day	Energy production, skin health	Cracked lips, sore throat	Rare
Vitamin B3 (Niacin)	Meat, fish, whole grains	14-16 mg/day	Energy production, DNA repair	Pellagra (diarrhea, dermatitis, dementia)	Flushing, liver damage
Vitamin B5 (Pantothenic Acid)	Meat, whole grains, broccoli	5 mg/day	Energy metabolism	Fatigue, irritability	Rare
Vitamin B6 (Pyridoxine)	Poultry, fish, bananas, potatoes	1.3-1.7 mg/day	Amino acid metabolism, neurotransmitter synthesis	Anemia, depression, confusion	Nerve damage, sensory neuropathy
Vitamin B7 (Biotin)	Eggs, nuts, seeds, sweet potatoes	30 µg/day	Fatty acid synthesis, energy metabolism	Hair loss, skin rash	Rare
Vitamin B9 (Folate)	Leafy greens, legumes, fortified cereals	400 µg/day	DNA synthesis, red blood cell formation	Neural tube defects, megaloblastic anemia	May mask B12 deficiency
Vitamin B12	Meat, fish, dairy, fortified cereals	2.4 µg/day	Red blood cell formation, nerve function	Pernicious anemia, neurological issues	Rare

Minerals

Mineral	Sources	Daily Requirement	Functions	Deficiency	Excess
Calcium	Dairy, leafy greens, fortified foods	1,000-1,200 mg/day	Bone health, muscle contraction, nerve signaling	Osteoporosis, muscle cramps	Kidney stones, impaired absorption of other minerals
Iron	Red meat, beans, spinach, fortified cereals	8-18 mg/day	Haemoglobin production, oxygen transport	Anaemia (fatigue, pallor, weakness)	Iron toxicity, organ damage
Magnesium	Nuts, seeds, whole grains, leafy greens	310-420 mg/day	Muscle function, nerve transmission	Muscle cramps, arrhythmias	Diarrhea, kidney issues
Potassium	Bananas, oranges, potatoes, spinach	2,600-3,400 mg/day	Fluid balance, muscle contraction	Weakness, irregular heartbeat	Hyperkalemia (heart issues)
Sodium	Table salt, processed foods	<2,300 mg/day	Fluid balance, nerve signaling	Rare (hyponatremia: nausea, fatigue)	Hypertension, fluid retention
Zinc	Meat, shellfish, legumes, nuts	8-11 mg/day	Immune function, wound healing	Impaired immunity, slow wound healing	Nausea, impaired absorption of copper
Iodine	Iodized salt, seafood, dairy	150 µg/day	Thyroid hormone production	Goiter, hypothyroidism	Thyroid dysfunction

Mineral	Sources	Daily Requirement	Functions	Deficiency	Excess
Phosphorus	Meat, dairy, nuts, whole grains	700 mg/day	Bone health, energy metabolism	Weakness, bone pain	Calcium imbalance, kidney damage
Fluoride	Fluoridated water, tea, fish	3-4 mg/day	Tooth enamel strength	Dental cavities	Fluorosis (discolored teeth)
Selenium	Seafood, nuts, eggs	55 µg/day	Antioxidant, thyroid function	Muscle pain, heart disease	Hair loss, nail brittleness

This table summarizes the essential vitamins and minerals, their sources, daily requirements, roles in the body, and the effects of deficiency and excess. Maintaining a balanced diet ensures proper intake of these nutrients for optimal health.

Chapter – 4

(4.1) General introduction to nervous system

General Introduction to the Nervous System

The nervous system is a complex network that serves as the body's command center, coordinating all voluntary and involuntary actions. It is responsible for processing sensory information, controlling movements, and regulating bodily functions. The nervous system can be divided into two main parts:

1. Central Nervous System (CNS) : Comprising the brain and spinal cord, the CNS processes information and coordinates responses.

2. Peripheral Nervous System (PNS) : Consisting of all the nerves outside the CNS, the PNS connects the CNS to the rest of the body. It is further divided into:

- Afferent Division : Carries sensory information to the CNS.
- Efferent Division : Transmits motor commands from the CNS to muscles and glands.

Neurons: The Functional Units of the Nervous System

Neurons are specialized cells that transmit nerve impulses throughout the nervous system. They consist of three main components:

- **Cell Body (Soma) :** Contains the nucleus and organelles, serving as the metabolic centre of the neuron.
- **Dendrites :** Branch-like structures that receive signals from other neurons and convey them toward the cell body.
- **Axon :** A long, thin fiber that transmits electrical impulses away from the cell body to other neurons or target tissues.

Neurons communicate through synapses, where neurotransmitters are released to transmit signals across gaps between neurons.

Mechanism of Propagation of Nerve Impulse

The propagation of a nerve impulse involves several key processes:

1. Resting Membrane Potential : Neurons maintain a resting membrane potential of approximately -70 mV due to differences in ion concentrations inside and outside the cell, primarily involving sodium (Na^+) and potassium (K^+) ions.

2. Depolarization : When a neuron is stimulated by a signal (such as from another neuron), sodium channels open, allowing Na^+ ions to flow into the neuron. This influx causes depolarization, making the inside of the neuron more positive.

3. Action Potential : If depolarization reaches a certain threshold (around -55 mV), an action potential is generated. This is an all-or-nothing response where voltage-gated sodium channels open rapidly, causing a rapid rise in membrane potential.

4. Repolarization : After reaching its peak (around +30 mV), sodium channels close, and potassium channels open. K^+ ions flow out of the neuron, restoring the negative membrane potential.

5. Hyperpolarization : The membrane potential may temporarily become more negative than resting potential due to prolonged potassium channel activity before returning to resting levels.

6. Propagation Along Axon : The action potential travels along the axon via saltatory conduction in myelinated neurons, where it jumps between nodes of Ranvier. This increases conduction speed compared to unmyelinated axons.

7. Transmission at Synapse: When the action potential reaches the axon terminal, it triggers the release of neurotransmitters into the synaptic cleft, allowing communication with adjacent neurons or target cells.

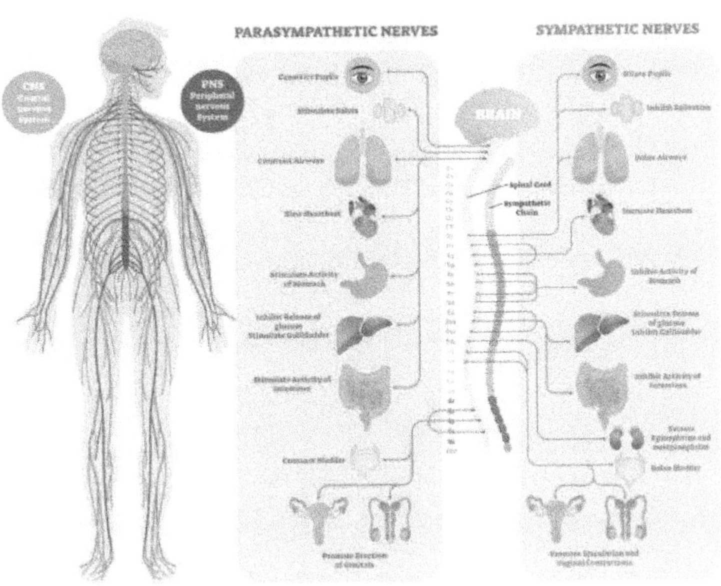

(4.2) Physiology of CNS, PNS, ANS

Physiology of the Central Nervous System (CNS), Peripheral Nervous System (PNS), and Autonomic Nervous System (ANS)

The nervous system is a complex and highly organized network responsible for coordinating bodily functions, processing sensory information, and facilitating communication between different body parts. It is divided into three main components: the Central Nervous System (CNS), Peripheral Nervous System (PNS), and Autonomic Nervous System (ANS). Each component has distinct structures and functions.

1. Central Nervous System (CNS)

Components :

The CNS consists of the brain and spinal cord, which are protected by bony structures (the skull and vertebral column) and three layers of protective membranes known as meninges.

- **Brain :** The brain is divided into several regions, including:
  - Cerebrum : Responsible for higher cognitive functions, sensory perception, and voluntary motor control. It is divided into lobes (frontal, parietal, temporal, occipital) that specialize in different functions.
  - Cerebellum : Coordinates balance and fine motor skills.
  - Brainstem : Controls basic life functions such as breathing, heart rate, and blood pressure. It includes the midbrain, pons, and medulla oblongata.

- **Spinal Cord :** Extends from the brainstem down the vertebral column. It serves as a conduit for signals between the brain and the rest of the body. The spinal cord contains both Gray matter (neuronal cell bodies) and white matter (myelinated axons) organized into ascending and descending tracts.

Functions :

- **Information Processing :** The CNS receives sensory input from the PNS, processes this information, and generates appropriate responses.

- **Motor Control :** Sends motor commands to skeletal muscles via motor neurons to facilitate movement.

- **Homeostasis Regulation :** Controls autonomic functions such as heart rate, blood pressure, digestion, and respiratory rate through reflex arcs.

2. Peripheral Nervous System (PNS)

Components :

The PNS includes all the nerves outside the CNS. It is subdivided into:

- **Somatic Nervous System (SNS) :** Controls voluntary movements by innervating skeletal muscles. It also transmits sensory information from peripheral receptors to the CNS.
- **Autonomic Nervous System (ANS) :** Regulates involuntary functions by controlling smooth muscles, cardiac muscles, and glands.

Functions :

- **Sensory Input :** The PNS carries sensory information from receptors in the skin, muscles, joints, and organs to the CNS.
- **Motor Output :** Transmits motor commands from the CNS to skeletal muscles via somatic motor neurons.

3. Autonomic Nervous System (ANS)

Components :

The ANS is further divided into:

- **Sympathetic Nervous System :** Prepares the body for "fight or flight" responses during stressful situations by increasing heart rate, dilating bronchioles, inhibiting digestion, and mobilizing energy stores.
- **Parasympathetic Nervous System :** Promotes "rest and digest" activities that conserve energy by slowing heart rate, enhancing digestive processes, and facilitating relaxation.

Functions :

- Sympathetic Division :
  - Increases heart rate and blood flow to muscles.
  - Dilates pupils for improved vision.
  - Inhibits gastrointestinal activity.

- Parasympathetic Division :
  - Decreases heart rate.
  - Stimulates digestive processes.
  - Promotes relaxation of sphincters in the gastrointestinal tract.

Mechanism of Propagation of Nerve Impulse

The propagation of nerve impulses involves several key steps:

1. Resting Membrane Potential : Neurons maintain a resting membrane potential of approximately -70 mV due to differences in ion concentrations across the membrane, primarily involving sodium (Na^+) and potassium (K^+).

2. Depolarization : When a neuron is stimulated by a signal (such as from another neuron), sodium channels open, allowing Na^+ ions to flow into the neuron. This influx causes depolarization.

3. Action Potential Generation : If depolarization reaches a certain threshold (~-55 mV), an action potential is generated. This involves rapid opening of voltage-gated sodium channels followed by their closure.

4. Repolarization : After reaching its peak (~+30 mV), sodium channels close while potassium channels open. K^+ ions exit the neuron, restoring a negative membrane potential.

5. Propagation Along Axon : The action potential travels along the axon via saltatory conduction in myelinated neurons, where it jumps between nodes of Ranvier. This increases conduction speed compared to unmyelinated axons.

6. Synaptic Transmission : When the action potential reaches the axon terminal, it triggers the release of neurotransmitters into the synaptic cleft, facilitating communication with adjacent neurons or target cells.

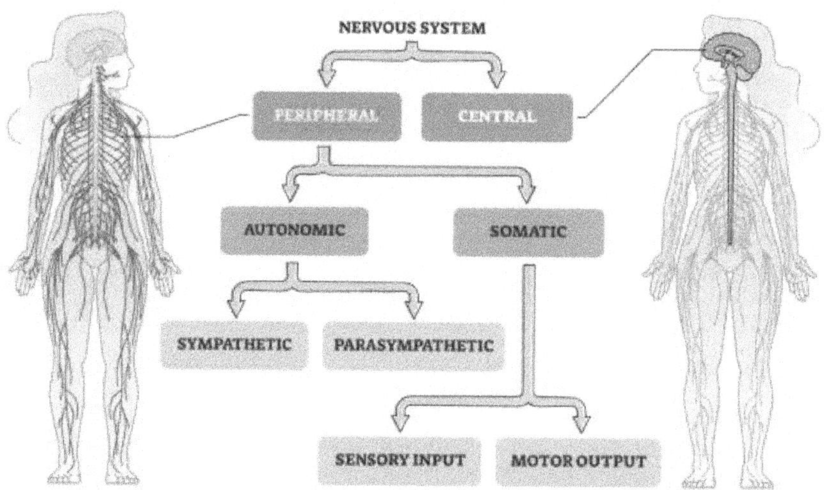

(4.3) Physiology of sensory and motor nervous system

The nervous system is a complex network responsible for processing sensory information and coordinating motor responses. It consists of two main functional divisions: the sensory nervous system, which detects and transmits sensory stimuli, and the motor nervous system, which executes voluntary and involuntary movements. Below is a detailed overview of both systems.

1. Sensory Nervous System

Function : The sensory nervous system is responsible for receiving external and internal stimuli through specialized sensory receptors and transmitting this information to the central nervous system (CNS) for processing.

Components :
- Sensory Receptors : Specialized cells that detect specific types of stimuli (e.g., light, sound, pressure, temperature, pain). These receptors can be classified into several categories:
  - Mechanoreceptors : Respond to mechanical forces (touch, pressure, vibration).
  - Thermoreceptors : Detect changes in temperature.
  - Photoreceptors : Respond to light (e.g., rods and cones in the retina).
  - Chemoreceptors : Detect chemical stimuli (taste and smell).
  - Nociceptors : Respond to pain stimuli.

Mechanism of Sensory Signal Transmission

1. Transduction : Sensory receptors convert stimuli into electrical signals (action potentials). This process involves depolarization of the receptor membrane when a stimulus exceeds a threshold level.

2. Ascending Pathways : Sensory information travels from peripheral receptors to the CNS via two main pathways:
- Spinothalamic Pathway : Transmits pain and temperature sensations. Primary sensory neurons synapse in the spinal cord before ascending to the thalamus.
- Dorsal Column-Medial Lemniscus Pathway : Carries fine touch, pressure, and proprioceptive information. Primary sensory neurons ascend ipsilaterally to the medulla before crossing over to synapse in the thalamus.

3. Processing in the CNS : The thalamus relays sensory information to the appropriate areas of the cerebral cortex for interpretation. For example, the somatosensory cortex processes tactile information, while the visual cortex processes visual stimuli.

2. Motor Nervous System

Function : The motor nervous system is responsible for executing voluntary and involuntary movements by transmitting commands from the CNS to muscles and glands.

Components :

- **Upper Motor Neurons (UMNs) :** Located in the brain and spinal cord, UMNs originate in the motor cortex or brainstem and send signals down to lower motor neurons.
- **Lower Motor Neurons (LMNs):** Located in the anterior horn of the spinal cord or brainstem nuclei, LMNs directly innervate skeletal muscles.

Types of Motor Responses :

- Voluntary Movements : Controlled by conscious thought processes involving UMNs originating in the motor cortex. These movements are typically learned and refined through practice.
- Reflex Movements : Involuntary responses mediated by reflex arcs that do not require conscious thought. For example, when touching a hot surface, sensory neurons transmit signals to interneurons in the spinal cord, which quickly activate LMNs to withdraw the hand before pain is consciously perceived.

Integration of Sensory and Motor Systems

The sensory and motor systems work together seamlessly:
- Sensory input informs the CNS about environmental conditions or internal states.
- The CNS processes this information and formulates an appropriate response.
- Motor commands are executed through LMNs that stimulate muscle contractions or glandular secretions.

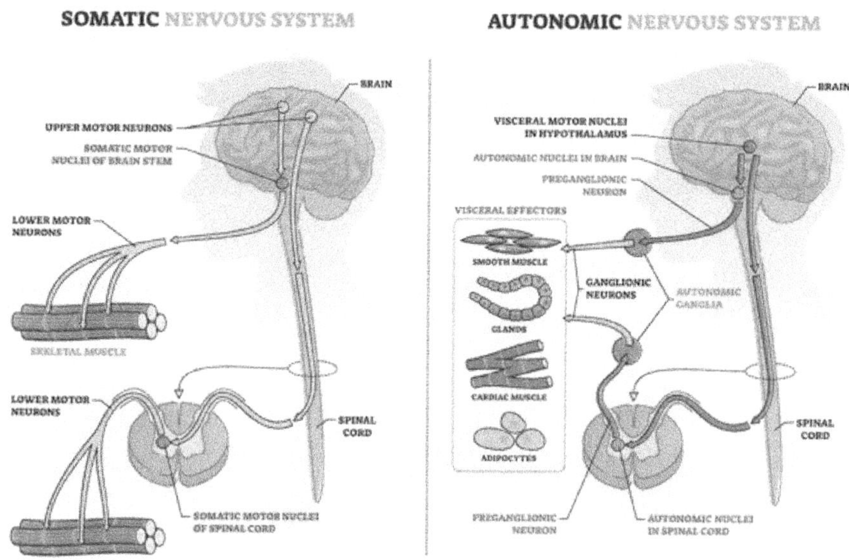

(4.4) Functions of different parts of brain and physiology of special senses, intelligence, memory, learning and motivation.

Functions of Different Parts of the Brain

The human brain is a highly complex organ divided into several regions, each responsible for specific functions. Here's an overview of the major parts of the brain and their roles:

1. Cerebrum

- **Frontal Lobe :**
  - **Functions :** Involved in higher cognitive functions such as reasoning, problem-solving, planning, and decision-making. It also controls voluntary motor functions and regulates emotions and personality traits.
  - **Key Areas :** Contains Broca's area (speech production) and the primary motor cortex (controls movement).

- **Parietal Lobe :**
  - **Functions :** Processes sensory information related to touch, temperature, pain, and proprioception (awareness of body position). It plays a role in spatial awareness and language comprehension.
  - **Key Areas :** Houses Wernicke's area, which is critical for understanding spoken language.

- **Temporal Lobe :**
  - **Functions :** Responsible for processing auditory information and is involved in memory formation and emotional responses. It plays a significant role in language comprehension.
  - **Key Areas :** Contains the hippocampus (memory formation) and the amygdala (emotion regulation).

- **Occipital Lobe :**
  - **Functions :** Primarily responsible for visual processing. It interprets visual information such as colour, shape, and motion.

2. Cerebellum

- **Functions :** Coordinates voluntary movements, balance, posture, and motor learning. It integrates sensory information to fine-tune motor activity and ensure smooth execution of movements.

3. Brainstem

- **Components :** Comprises the midbrain, pons, and medulla oblongata.
- **Functions :**
  - **Midbrain :** Involved in vision, hearing, motor control, sleep/wake cycles, arousal, and temperature regulation.

- **Pons :** Connects different parts of the brain; involved in regulating breathing and relaying signals between the cerebellum and cerebrum.
- **Medulla Oblongata :** Controls autonomic functions such as heart rate, blood pressure, respiration, and reflexes like swallowing and vomiting.

4. Thalamus

- **Functions:** Acts as a relay station for sensory information (except smell) to the cerebral cortex. It plays a role in regulating consciousness, sleep, and alertness.

5. Limbic System

- **Components :** Includes structures such as the hippocampus and amygdala.
- **Functions :**
  - **Hippocampus :** Essential for memory formation and spatial navigation.
  - **Amygdala :** Involved in emotional processing, fear response, and memory consolidation related to emotions.

Physiology of Special Senses

The special senses include vision, hearing, taste, smell, and balance. Each sense has specialized receptors that transduce stimuli into neural signals:

1. Vision :
- Photoreceptors (rods and cones) in the retina convert light into electrical impulses.
- Signals are processed in the visual cortex located in the occipital lobe.

2. Hearing :
- Sound waves are detected by hair cells in the cochlea of the inner ear.
- Neural signals are transmitted to the auditory cortex in the temporal lobe for processing.

3. Taste (Gustation) :
- Taste buds on the tongue detect chemical substances (sweet, sour, salty, bitter, umami).
- Signals are relayed to the gustatory cortex for interpretation.

4. Smell (Olfaction) :
- Olfactory receptors in the nasal cavity detect airborne chemicals.
- Signals are sent directly to the olfactory bulb and then to areas involved in emotion and memory.

5. Balance (Vestibular System) :
- The inner ear contains structures (semi-circular canals) that detect changes in head position and movement.
- Information is integrated with visual input to maintain balance.

Intelligence, Memory, Learning, and Motivation

Intelligence

- Intelligence involves cognitive processes such as reasoning, problem-solving, abstract thinking, and adaptability. The frontal lobe plays a crucial role in these higher-order functions.

Memory

- Memory is categorized into short-term (working) memory and long-term memory. The hippocampus is vital for forming new memories while other areas of the cerebral cortex store long-term memories.

Learning

- Learning involves acquiring new knowledge or skills through experience or education. It requires synaptic plasticity—changes in synapse strength—which is facilitated by neurotransmitters like glutamate.

Motivation

- Motivation is driven by neural circuits involving the limbic system (especially the amygdala) and prefrontal cortex. Dopamine pathways play a significant role in reward processing and reinforcing behaviours that lead to positive outcomes.

(4.5) Physiology of sleep and dreams

Physiology of Sleep and Dreams

Sleep is a complex physiological state characterized by altered consciousness, reduced sensory activity, inhibition of voluntary muscles, and decreased interactions with the environment. It plays a crucial role in physical health, cognitive function, and emotional well-being. The sleep cycle consists of various stages that contribute to restorative processes in the body.

1. Stages of Sleep

Sleep is divided into two main phases: Non-Rapid Eye Movement (NREM) and Rapid Eye Movement (REM) sleep. Each phase is further divided into stages:

- NREM Sleep : Comprises three stages (N1, N2, N3).

- Stage N1 (Light Sleep) :
- Duration : Lasts about 1-7 minutes.
- Physiological Changes : Transition from wakefulness to sleep; characterized by theta waves in EEG readings. Muscle tone decreases, and eye movements are slow.
- Function : Acts as a bridge between wakefulness and deeper sleep; easy to awaken during this stage.

- Stage N2 (Moderate Sleep) :
- Duration : Lasts approximately 10-25 minutes in the first cycle and increases with subsequent cycles.
- Physiological Changes : Heart rate and body temperature drop; EEG shows sleep spindles and K-complexes. Eye movements cease.
- Function : Facilitates memory consolidation and learning; about 45% of total sleep time is spent in this stage.

- Stage N3 (Deep Sleep) :
- Duration : Typically lasts 20-40 minutes.
- Physiological Changes : Characterized by delta waves in EEG readings, indicating deep sleep. Breathing and heart rate are at their lowest.
- Function : Vital for physical restoration, tissue repair, growth, and immune function; difficult to awaken during this stage.

- REM Sleep :
- Duration : First REM period lasts about 10 minutes but increases with each cycle throughout the night.
- **Physiological Changes :** Rapid eye movements occur behind closed eyelids; brain activity resembles that of wakefulness (beta waves). Heart rate and blood pressure increase; muscle atonia occurs (temporary paralysis of most voluntary muscles).
- **Function :** Associated with vivid dreaming; plays a critical role in emotional regulation, memory consolidation, and creativity.

2. Sleep Cycle

A typical sleep cycle lasts approximately 90 to 110 minutes, with individuals cycling through NREM and REM stages multiple times per night (about 4 to 6 cycles). As the night progresses, the duration of REM sleep increases while deep NREM sleep decreases.

Physiology of Dreams

Dreams primarily occur during REM sleep when brain activity is high. The exact physiological mechanisms underlying dreaming are not fully understood, but several theories exist:

- Memory Consolidation : Dreams may play a role in processing memories and emotions from daily experiences.
- Problem Solving : Some researchers suggest that dreams facilitate creative problem-solving by allowing the brain to explore different scenarios without real-world constraints.
- Emotional Regulation : Dreams may help process emotions and experiences, contributing to psychological well-being.

Importance of Sleep

Sleep is essential for various physiological functions:

- **Physical Restoration :** Growth hormone is released during deep sleep, promoting tissue repair and growth.
- **Cognitive Function :** Adequate sleep enhances learning, memory retention, and cognitive performance. Sleep deprivation can impair attention, decision-making, and problem-solving abilities.
- **Emotional Health :** Quality sleep contributes to emotional stability; insufficient sleep is linked to mood disorders such as anxiety and depression.

(4.6) EEG

Electroencephalogram (EEG): Overview

An electroencephalogram (EEG) is a diagnostic test that measures the electrical activity of the brain. It is widely used in clinical settings to assess brain function and diagnose various neurological conditions. Here's a detailed overview based on the search results.

What is an EEG?

- **Definition :** An EEG records the spontaneous electrical activity of the brain through electrodes placed on the scalp. These electrodes detect electrical impulses produced by neuronal activity, primarily from pyramidal neurons in the cerebral cortex.

- **Purpose :** EEGs are primarily used to diagnose conditions such as epilepsy, sleep disorders, head injuries, brain tumours, and encephalopathies. They help in understanding brain function and identifying abnormalities in electrical activity.

Procedure

- **Electrode Placement :** Small metal discs called electrodes are attached to the scalp using a conductive gel or paste. The placement follows a standardized system known as the International 10–20 system, which ensures consistent positioning for accurate readings.
- **Recording :** The electrodes measure electrical potentials generated by synchronized neuronal activity. The signals are transmitted to a computer that records them as wavy lines, representing different brain wave patterns (delta, theta, alpha, beta).
- **Duration :** The test typically lasts between 20 minutes to several hours, depending on the specific requirements (e.g., routine EEG vs. sleep-deprived EEG).

Types of Brain Waves

EEG recordings display various brain wave patterns, each associated with different states of consciousness:

- Delta Waves : Slow waves (0.5–4 Hz) seen during deep sleep.
- Theta Waves : Associated with light sleep and relaxation (4–8 Hz).
- Alpha Waves : Present during relaxed wakefulness (8–12 Hz).
- Beta Waves : Fast waves (12–30 Hz) associated with active thinking and alertness.

Clinical Applications

EEGs are utilized to diagnose and monitor several conditions:
- Seizure Disorders : Identifying types of seizures and their origins.
- Sleep Disorders : Assessing conditions like sleep apnoea and narcolepsy.
- Brain Injuries : Evaluating the extent of damage from trauma.
- Encephalitis : Detecting inflammation of the brain.
- Dementia and Cognitive Disorders : Monitoring changes in brain activity associated with neurodegenerative diseases.

Interpreting EEG Results

- Abnormal patterns such as spikes, sharp waves, or slow waves may indicate conditions like epilepsy or other neurological disorders.
- Normal brain activity typically shows rhythmic patterns with varying frequencies depending on the state of consciousness.

Risks and Considerations

EEGs are generally safe and non-invasive. However, some considerations include:
- Mild discomfort from electrode placement.
- Potential for misinterpretation of results due to artifacts from muscle activity or external interference.

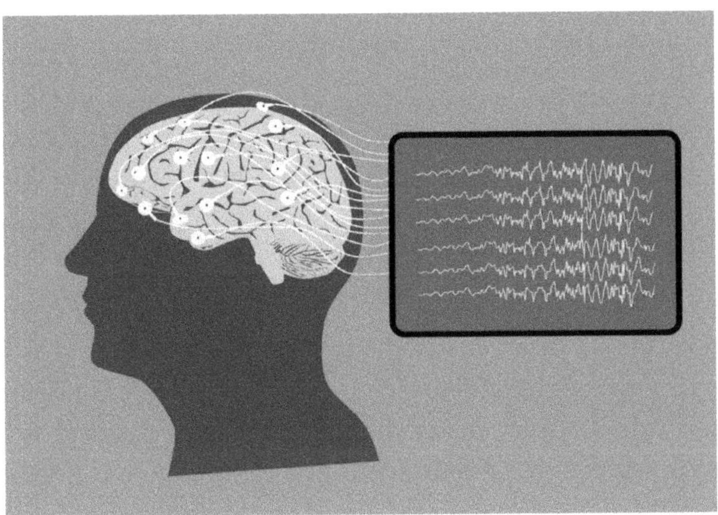

(4.7) Physiology of speech and articulation

Physiology of Speech and Articulation

The physiology of speech production involves complex interactions between various anatomical structures and physiological processes. Speech is generated through the coordinated actions of the respiratory system, larynx, and articulatory structures in the mouth and throat. Here's an overview of how these systems work together to produce speech.

1. Components of Speech Production

Speech production can be divided into three main processes: initiation, phonation, and articulation.

- **Initiation :**

- **Airflow Generation :** The process begins with the generation of airflow from the lungs. This is primarily achieved through the pulmonic airstream mechanism, where air is expelled from the lungs during exhalation.

- **Mechanisms :**
  - **Egressive Sounds :** Produced by exhaling air (e.g., saying "Hello").
  - **Ingressive Sounds :** Produced by inhaling air (less common in speech).

- **Phonation :**

- **Vocal Fold Vibration :** The airflow passes through the larynx, where the vocal folds (cords) are located. When air pressure builds up from the lungs, it causes the vocal folds to vibrate, producing sound waves.

- **Control of Pitch and Volume :** The tension and length of the vocal folds can be adjusted by laryngeal muscles, which modulate pitch (frequency) and volume (amplitude) of the sound produced.

- **Articulation :**

- **Modification of Sounds :** After phonation, the sound waves travel through the vocal tract, where they are shaped into distinct speech sounds by various articulators.
- **Articulators :** These include:
  - **Active Articulators :** Tongue, lower jaw, lips.
  - **Passive Articulators :** Hard palate, alveolar ridge, upper teeth.
  - **Resonance Chambers :** The pharyngeal, oral, and nasal cavities act as resonators that modify the sound quality. The configuration of these cavities determines the specific sounds produced.

2. Neural Control of Speech

Speech production is controlled by specific areas in the brain:

- **Broca's Area :** Located in the frontal lobe, this area is responsible for language production and motor control for speech. Damage to this area can result in Broca's aphasia, characterized by difficulty forming words while comprehension remains intact.

- **Wernicke's Area :** Located in the temporal lobe, this area is involved in language comprehension. Damage here can lead to Wernicke's aphasia, where individuals produce fluent but nonsensical speech.

- **Arcuate Fasciculus :** A bundle of nerve fibers connecting Broca's and Wernicke's areas, facilitating communication between language comprehension and production.

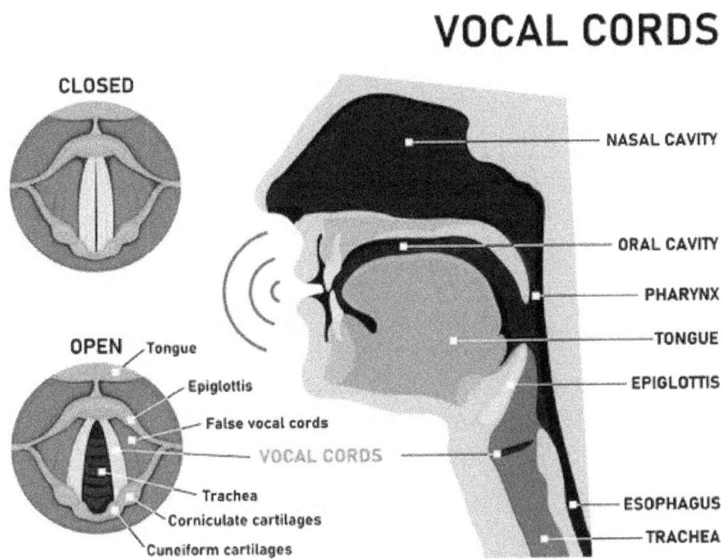

(4.8) Physiology of Temperature Regulation

Temperature regulation is a critical physiological process that maintains body temperature within a narrow range (approximately 36.1°C to 37.2°C or 97°F to 99°F). This homeostasis is essential for optimal enzyme function and overall metabolic processes.

1. Mechanisms of Temperature Regulation

The body employs several mechanisms to regulate temperature:

- Thermoregulation Centres :
- Located in the hypothalamus, these centres receive input from peripheral thermoreceptors (located in skin) and central thermoreceptors (located in core body regions).

- Heat Production :
- The body generates heat through metabolic processes (e.g., cellular respiration) and muscle activity (e.g., shivering). Hormones like thyroxine can increase metabolic rate and heat production.

- Heat Loss Mechanisms :
- **Radiation :** Heat loss through infrared radiation from the body surface.
- **Conduction :** Transfer of heat to cooler objects in direct contact with the skin.
- **Convection :** Heat loss through air or water movement around the body.
- **Evaporation :** Heat loss through sweat evaporation; this is a significant mechanism during exercise or high temperatures.

2. Responses to Temperature Changes

- Hyperthermia (Increased Body Temperature) :

- When body temperature rises above normal due to external heat or internal factors (e.g., fever), mechanisms such as increased sweating and vasodilation (widening of blood vessels) are activated to promote heat loss.

- Hypothermia (Decreased Body Temperature) :
- In cold environments or during prolonged exposure to low temperatures, mechanisms such as shivering (muscle contractions generating heat) and vasoconstriction (narrowing of blood vessels) are activated to conserve heat.

Chapter – 5

(5.1) General introduction to endocrine system

The endocrine system is a complex network of glands that produce and secrete hormones, which are chemical messengers that regulate various physiological processes in the body. Here's a comprehensive overview of the endocrine system, its components, functions, and significance.

Overview of the Endocrine System

Definition and Components

- **Endocrine Glands :** These are specialized organs that release hormones directly into the bloodstream without using ducts. Major endocrine glands include.

- **Pituitary Gland :** Often referred to as the "master gland," it regulates other endocrine glands and produces hormones such as growth hormone (GH) and adrenocorticotropic hormone (ACTH).

- **Thyroid Gland :** Produces hormones like thyroxine (T4) and triiodothyronine (T3), which regulate metabolism.

- **Adrenal Glands :** Comprised of the cortex and medulla, they produce hormones such as cortisol (stress response) and adrenaline (epinephrine).

- **Pancreas :** Functions as both an endocrine and exocrine gland; it produces insulin and glucagon to regulate blood sugar levels.

- **Gonads :** Ovaries in females produce oestrogen and progesterone, while testes in males produce testosterone, regulating reproductive functions.

Hormones

- Hormones are biochemical substances that travel through the bloodstream to target organs or tissues, where they bind to specific receptors to elicit a response. They play crucial roles in regulating:
  - Metabolism
  - Growth and development
  - Tissue function
  - Sexual function
  - Mood and stress responses

Functions of the Endocrine System

The endocrine system influences nearly every cell, organ, and function in the body. Key functions include:

1. Regulation of Metabolism : Hormones like insulin and glucagon from the pancreas regulate glucose metabolism, ensuring energy balance.
2. Growth and Development : Growth hormone from the pituitary gland promotes growth in children and adolescents.
3. Reproductive Functions : Gonadal hormones control sexual development, menstrual cycles in females, and sperm production in males.
4. Stress Response : The adrenal glands release cortisol and adrenaline in response to stress, preparing the body for "fight or flight" situations.
5. Homeostasis Maintenance : The endocrine system helps maintain homeostasis by regulating body temperature, fluid balance, and electrolyte levels.

Mechanisms of Hormonal Action

Hormones exert their effects through specific mechanisms:
- **Feedback Loops :** The endocrine system operates primarily through feedback mechanisms (negative or positive feedback) to maintain homeostasis. For example:
  - In negative feedback, an increase in hormone levels leads to a decrease in its production (e.g., high blood glucose stimulates insulin release, which lowers blood glucose levels).
- **Signal Transduction :** Hormones bind to receptors on target cells, triggering intracellular signalling pathways that result in physiological responses.

Importance of the Endocrine System

The proper functioning of the endocrine system is vital for overall health. Dysregulation can lead to various disorders.
- Diabetes Mellitus : Caused by insufficient insulin production or action.
- Thyroid Disorders : Such as hyperthyroidism or hypothyroidism affecting metabolism.
- Growth Disorders : Resulting from abnormal levels of growth hormone.

(5.2) Classification and characteristics of hormones

Classification and Characteristics of Hormones

Hormones are chemical messengers produced by various glands in the endocrine system, and they play crucial roles in regulating physiological processes throughout the body. They can be classified based on their chemical structure and solubility. Here's a detailed overview of the types of hormones and their characteristics.

1. Classification of Hormones

Hormones can be categorized into three main classes based on their chemical structure:

- **Lipid-Derived Hormones :**

- **Characteristics :** These hormones are derived from cholesterol and are lipophilic (fat-soluble), allowing them to easily diffuse across cell membranes.
- **Examples :**
- **Steroid Hormones :** Include testosterone, oestradiol, progesterone, cortisol, and aldosterone. They typically act on intracellular receptors to influence gene expression and cellular activity.
- **Function :** Regulate metabolism, immune function, salt and water balance, and reproductive functions.

- **Amino Acid-Derived Hormones :**

- **Characteristics :** These hormones are derived from single amino acids, primarily tyrosine and tryptophan. They can be either hydrophilic or lipophilic.
- **Examples :**
- **Catecholamines :** Such as epinephrine (adrenaline) and norepinephrine (noradrenaline), which are produced by the adrenal medulla.
- **Thyroid Hormones :** Thyroxine (T4) and triiodothyronine (T3), which regulate metabolism.
- **Melatonin :** Produced by the pineal gland, involved in regulating sleep-wake cycles.
- **Function :** Involved in stress responses, metabolic regulation, and circadian rhythms.

- **Peptide Hormones :**

- **Characteristics :** Composed of chains of amino acids, these hormones are generally hydrophilic (water-soluble) and cannot cross cell membranes easily. They are stored in vesicles within endocrine cells until needed.
- **Examples :**
- Insulin (produced by the pancreas), growth hormone (GH), antidiuretic hormone (ADH), and oxytocin.
- **Function :** Regulate a wide range of physiological processes including glucose metabolism, growth, fluid balance, and reproductive functions.

2. Mechanisms of Action

- Lipid-derived hormones typically enter target cells and bind to intracellular receptors, leading to changes in gene expression and protein synthesis.
- Amino acid-derived hormones and peptide hormones bind to specific receptors on the cell surface, triggering signal transduction pathways that result in rapid cellular responses.

3. Regulation of Hormone Secretion

Hormone secretion is tightly regulated through feedback mechanisms:
- **Negative Feedback :** The most common regulatory mechanism where an increase in hormone levels leads to a decrease in its production. For example, high blood glucose levels stimulate insulin release; once glucose levels normalize, insulin secretion decreases.
- **Positive Feedback :** Less common; an increase in hormone levels stimulates further production. An example is oxytocin during childbirth, where uterine contractions stimulate more oxytocin release until delivery occurs.

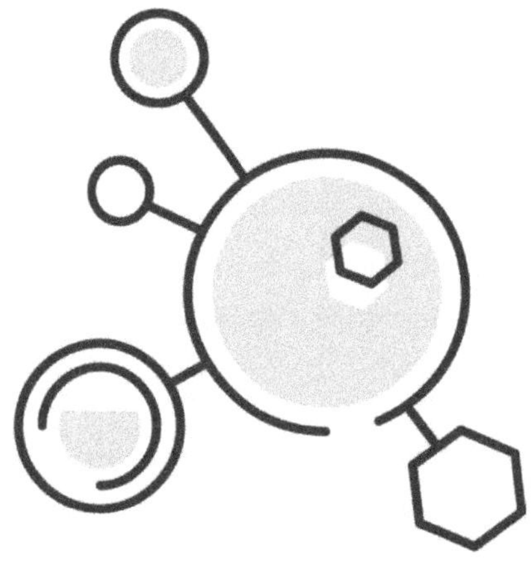

Hormones

(5.3) Physiology of all endocrine glands, their functions and their effects

Physiology of the Endocrine Glands: Functions and Effects

The endocrine system consists of various glands that produce hormones, which are chemical messengers that regulate numerous physiological processes in the body. Each gland has specific functions and effects that contribute to maintaining homeostasis, growth, metabolism, and overall health. Below is an overview of the major endocrine glands, their functions, and the effects of their hormones.

1. Hypothalamus

- **Function :** The hypothalamus is a critical regulatory centre located at the base of the brain. It produces hormones that control the pituitary gland and regulates various bodily functions.
- **Hormones:**
  - **Releasing Hormones :** Stimulate the release of hormones from the pituitary (e.g., Thyrotropin-releasing hormone (TRH), Gonadotropin-releasing hormone (GnRH)).
  - **Inhibiting Hormones :** Suppress hormone release from the pituitary (e.g., Somatostatin).
  - **Effects :** Regulates body temperature, hunger, thirst, sleep-wake cycles, and emotional responses.

2. Pituitary Gland

- **Function :** Often referred to as the "master gland," it controls other endocrine glands and regulates growth and metabolism.
- **Hormones :**
  - Growth Hormone (GH) : Stimulates growth and cell reproduction.
  - Prolactin (PRL) : Promotes milk production in breastfeeding.
  - Adrenocorticotropic Hormone (ACTH) : Stimulates adrenal glands to produce cortisol.
  - Thyroid-Stimulating Hormone (TSH) : Stimulates thyroid hormone production.
  - Luteinizing Hormone (LH) and Follicle-Stimulating Hormone (FSH) : Regulate reproductive processes.
  - Effects : Influences growth, metabolism, stress response, and reproductive functions.

3. Pineal Gland

- **Function :** Located in the brain, it regulates sleep patterns.
- **Hormones :**
  - Melatonin : Regulates circadian rhythms and sleep-wake cycles.
  - Effects : Promotes sleepiness during dark periods and helps regulate seasonal biological rhythms.

4. Thyroid Gland

- **Function :** Located in the neck, it plays a crucial role in metabolism.

- **Hormones :**
  - Thyroxine (T4) and Triiodothyronine (T3) : Regulate metabolic rate, heart rate, and growth.
  - Calcitonin : Helps regulate calcium levels in the blood by promoting calcium deposition in bones.
  - Effects : Increases energy expenditure; influences growth and development; maintains healthy bones.

5. Parathyroid Glands

- **Function :** Small glands located behind the thyroid gland that regulate calcium levels.
- **Hormones :**
  - Parathyroid Hormone (PTH) : Increases blood calcium levels by promoting calcium release from bones and increasing intestinal absorption of calcium.
  - Effects : Maintains calcium homeostasis; essential for bone health.

6. Thymus

- **Function :** Located in the upper chest; plays a role in immune function.
- **Hormones :**
  - Thymosin : Promotes the development of T lymphocytes (T cells), which are crucial for adaptive immunity.
  - Effects : Essential for immune system development, especially during childhood.

7. Adrenal Glands

- **Function :** Located atop each kidney; involved in stress response and metabolism regulation.
- **Hormones :**
  - Cortisol (glucocorticoid): Involved in stress response, metabolism regulation, and immune function suppression.
  - Aldosterone (mineralocorticoid): Regulates sodium and potassium balance; influences blood pressure.
  - Catecholamines (e.g., Epinephrine and Norepinephrine): Prepare the body for "fight or flight" responses during stress.
  - Effects : Regulates metabolism, blood pressure, heart rate, and stress responses.

8. Pancreas

- **Function :** Functions as both an endocrine and exocrine gland; regulates blood sugar levels.
- **Hormones :**
  - Insulin : Lowers blood glucose levels by facilitating glucose uptake into cells.
  - Glucagon : Raises blood glucose levels by promoting glycogen breakdown in the liver.
  - Effects : Maintains glucose homeostasis; essential for energy metabolism.

9. Gonads (Ovaries and Testes)

- **Function :** Responsible for producing sex hormones that regulate reproductive functions.
- **Hormones :**
  - In Ovaries:

- Oestrogen : Regulates menstrual cycle, secondary sexual characteristics, and reproductive health.
- Progesterone : Prepares the uterus for pregnancy and maintains early pregnancy.
- In Testes:
- Testosterone : Promotes sperm production and secondary sexual characteristics in males.
- Effects : Influence sexual development, reproductive processes, and overall sexual health.

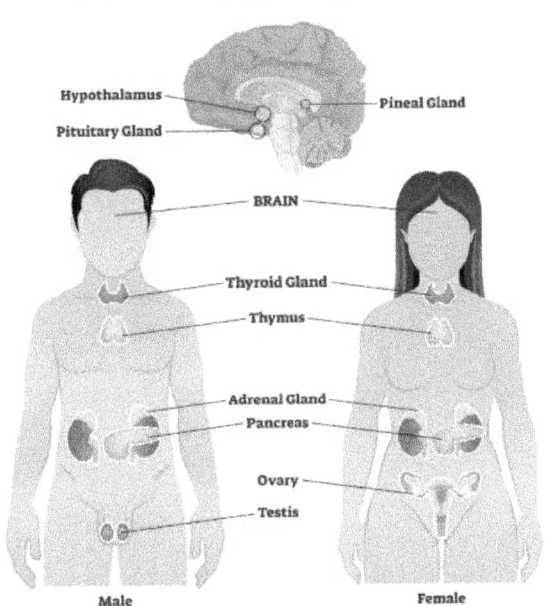

Chapter – 6

(6.1) Composition, Functions of blood and blood cells, Haemopoiesis (stages and development of RBCs, and WBCs and platelets)

Blood is a vital fluid connective tissue that plays critical roles in maintaining homeostasis and supporting various physiological functions in the body. It consists of plasma and formed elements, which include red blood cells (RBCs), white blood cells (WBCs), and platelets. Here's a detailed overview of the composition, functions, and the process of hemopoiesis.

1. Composition of Blood

Blood is composed of two main components:

Blood is a complex bodily fluid that consists of several components, each playing a vital role in maintaining health and homeostasis. The major components of blood are:

1. Plasma

- **Percentage:** About 55% of blood volume
- **Composition:** Plasma is a yellowish liquid that contains:
    - **Water (90%)** – Acts as a solvent for carrying other components.
    - **Proteins** – Such as albumin (regulates osmotic pressure), globulins (antibodies and transport), and fibrinogen (important for blood clotting).
    - **Electrolytes** – Such as sodium, potassium, calcium, and bicarbonate, which help maintain fluid balance, pH, and muscle function.
    - **Nutrients** – Glucose, amino acids, and lipids.
    - **Waste products** – Such as urea and creatinine, which are excreted by the kidneys.
    - **Hormones** – Regulatory substances secreted by various glands.
    - **Gases** – Oxygen and carbon dioxide (though most oxygen is carried by red blood cells).

2. Red Blood Cells (RBCs) or Erythrocytes

- **Percentage:** About 45% of blood volume
- **Function:** The primary role of RBCs is to transport oxygen from the lungs to the tissues and return carbon dioxide from the tissues back to the lungs.
- **Composition:** Contain the protein **haemoglobin**, which binds to oxygen and carbon dioxide. RBCs lack a nucleus and have a biconcave shape to maximize surface area for gas exchange.

3. White Blood Cells (WBCs) or Leukocytes

- **Percentage:** Less than 1% of blood volume
- **Function:** WBCs are crucial for immune defence. They are involved in recognizing and responding to pathogens, infections, and foreign substances. There are five main types of white blood cells:
    - **Neutrophils** – First responders to bacterial infection.
    - **Lymphocytes** – Involved in adaptive immunity (B cells, T cells, and natural killer cells).
    - **Monocytes** – Become macrophages and help in cleaning up debris and pathogens.
    - **Eosinophils** – Involved in allergic reactions and parasitic infections.
    - **Basophils** – Release histamine in allergic reactions and inflammation.

4. Platelets or Thrombocytes

- **Percentage:** Less than 1% of blood volume
- **Function:** Platelets play a key role in blood clotting and wound healing by aggregating at the site of injury and forming a clot to prevent excessive blood loss.

Blood Cell Count and Haematocrit:

- **Haematocrit**: The percentage of blood volume that is made up of red blood cells. In healthy adults, it typically ranges from 40-45%.
- **Normal Blood Counts**:
    - RBC count: 4.7 to 6.1 million cells/μL for men, 4.2 to 5.4 million cells/μL for women.
    - WBC count: 4,000 to 11,000 cells/μL.
    - Platelet count: 150,000 to 450,000 cells/μL.

Blood composition can vary slightly depending on age, gender, hydration, and overall health.

2. Functions of Blood

Blood performs several critical functions:

- Transport :
- Carries oxygen from the lungs to tissues and carbon dioxide from tissues to the lungs for exhalation.
- Transports nutrients from the digestive tract to cells throughout the body.
- Removes waste products from metabolism for excretion by the kidneys and lungs.
- Delivers hormones from endocrine glands to target organs.

- Regulation :
- Maintains homeostasis by regulating body temperature through heat distribution.
- Helps regulate pH levels through buffers present in plasma.
- Maintains fluid balance by controlling osmotic pressure.

- **Protection :**
  - White blood cells defend against infections by identifying and destroying pathogens.
  - Antibodies in plasma provide immune protection against foreign substances.
  - Platelets initiate blood clotting to prevent excessive bleeding following injury.

3. Hemopoiesis

Hemopoiesis is the process of blood cell formation that occurs primarily in the bone marrow. It involves the development of erythrocytes (RBCs), leukocytes (WBCs), and platelets from hematopoietic stem cells.

- Stages of Development :

A. Red Blood Cells (Erythropoiesis) :
- Begins with hematopoietic stem cells differentiating into erythroid progenitor cells.
- Progenitor cells mature into erythroblasts, which synthesize haemoglobin.
- Erythroblasts lose their nuclei to become reticulocytes before entering circulation as mature RBCs.

B. White Blood Cells (Leukopoiesis) :
- Hematopoietic stem cells differentiate into various progenitor cells depending on the type of WBC being produced:
  - Myeloid Lineage : Produces neutrophils, eosinophils, basophils, monocytes.
  - Lymphoid Lineage : Produces lymphocytes (T cells and B cells).
  - Each type undergoes specific maturation processes influenced by growth factors.

C. Platelets (Thrombopoiesis) :
- Megakaryocytes in the bone marrow undergo endomitosis to become large multinucleated cells.
- Fragmentation of megakaryocytes releases platelets into circulation.

(6.2) Composition and functions of bone marrow

Composition and Functions of Bone Marrow

Bone marrow is a vital tissue found within the cavities of bones, playing a crucial role in the production of blood cells and maintaining overall health. It consists of two primary types: red marrow and yellow marrow, each with distinct functions and characteristics.

1. Composition of Bone Marrow

- Red Bone Marrow :

- **Hematopoietic Stem Cells :** These are multipotent stem cells responsible for the formation of all blood cells, including red blood cells (RBCs), white blood cells (WBCs), and platelets.
- Stromal Cells : These supportive cells include fibroblasts, macrophages, adipocytes, and endothelial cells that create a microenvironment conducive to haematopoiesis (blood cell formation).
- Matrix Components : The extracellular matrix consists of collagen, glycosaminoglycans, and other proteins that provide structural support and facilitate cell interactions.

- Yellow Bone Marrow :

- **Adipocytes :** Composed primarily of fat cells, yellow marrow serves as an energy reserve.
- **Inactive Hematopoietic Tissue :** Contains fewer hematopoietic stem cells compared to red marrow; however, it can revert to red marrow under certain conditions (e.g., significant blood loss).

2. Functions of Bone Marrow

- Haematopoiesis : The primary function of red bone marrow is the production of blood cells. This process includes:
  - Erythropoiesis : The formation of RBCs, which transport oxygen throughout the body.
  - Leukopoiesis : The production of WBCs, which are essential for immune defence against infections.
  - Thrombopoiesis : The generation of platelets, which are crucial for blood clotting.

- Storage of Fat : Yellow bone marrow stores fat that can be utilized as an energy source when needed.

- Support for Immune Function : Bone marrow produces various immune cells that play roles in both innate and adaptive immunity.

(6.3) Structure, types and functions of haemoglobin

Structure of Haemoglobin

Haemoglobin (Hb) is a globular metalloprotein with a quaternary structure, composed of four subunits: two alpha (α) and two beta (β) chains, each associated with a heme group. The overall molecular weight of haemoglobin is approximately 64,000 Daltons. Each alpha chain consists of 141 amino acids, while each beta chain contains 146 amino acids.

Heme Group

The heme group is a porphyrin ring that contains an iron (Fe^{2+}) ion at its centre, which is crucial for oxygen binding. Each haemoglobin molecule can bind up to four oxygen molecules, as it contains four heme groups. The heme is covalently attached to the globin protein via the imidazole ring of a histidine residue, allowing for reversible binding with oxygen.

Quaternary Structure

Haemoglobin's quaternary structure arises from the arrangement of its four subunits in a tetrahedral formation. The polypeptide chains fold into alpha-helices connected by non-helical segments, stabilized by hydrogen bonds. This folding creates pockets that effectively bind the heme groups.

Types of Haemoglobin

There are several types of haemoglobin, primarily categorized based on their subunit composition:

- **Haemoglobin A (HbA) :** The most common type in adults, composed of two alpha and two beta chains ($\alpha_2\beta_2$).
- **Haemoglobin A2 (HbA2) :** Comprising two alpha and two delta chains ($\alpha_2\delta_2$), it accounts for about 2-3% of adult haemoglobin.
- **Fetal Haemoglobin (HbF) :** Found in foetuses and new-borns, made up of two alpha and two gamma chains ($\alpha_2\gamma_2$), HbF has a higher affinity for oxygen than HbA.
- **Abnormal Haemoglobins**: Variants such as Haemoglobin S (associated with sickle cell anaemia) and Haemoglobin E also exist due to mutations in the globin genes.

Functions of Haemoglobin

The primary functions of haemoglobin include:

1. Oxygen Transport : Haemoglobin carries oxygen from the lungs to tissues. When oxygen binds to haemoglobin, it forms oxyhaemoglobin; when it releases oxygen, it becomes deoxyhaemoglobin. Approximately 98% of oxygen in blood is transported this way.

2. Carbon Dioxide Transport : Haemoglobin also transports carbon dioxide from tissues back to the lungs. When carbon dioxide binds to haemoglobin, it forms carbaminohaemoglobin, which accounts for about 25% of carbon dioxide transport in the blood.

3. pH Buffering : Haemoglobin plays a role in maintaining blood pH by buffering hydrogen ions produced during metabolic processes.

4. Cooperative Binding : The binding of oxygen to haemoglobin exhibits cooperative behaviour; the binding of one oxygen molecule increases the affinity for subsequent oxygen molecules due to conformational changes in the protein structure.

In summary, haemoglobin's structure enables it to efficiently transport oxygen and carbon dioxide while also contributing to acid-base balance in the blood.

Structure of hemoglobin

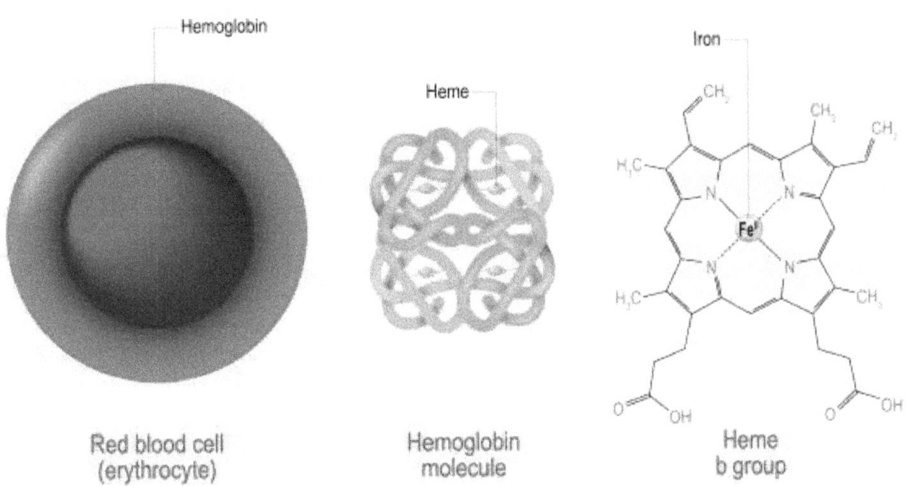

(6.4) Mechanism of blood clotting

The mechanism of blood clotting, or coagulation, is a complex process that involves multiple steps and pathways to prevent excessive bleeding following vascular injury. It can be divided into two main stages: primary hemostasis and secondary hemostasis.

Primary Hemostasis

This initial stage involves the formation of a weak platelet plug at the site of injury and includes four key phases:

1. Vasoconstriction : Immediately after a blood vessel is injured, vasoconstriction occurs to reduce blood flow. This response is primarily mediated by endothelin-1, released from damaged endothelial cells.

2. Platelet Adhesion : Platelets adhere to the exposed subendothelial collagen and von Willebrand factor (vWF) at the injury site. vWF acts as a bridge between platelets and the collagen fibers.

3. Platelet Activation : Adhered platelets undergo activation, changing shape and releasing chemical signals that recruit additional platelets to the site of injury.

4. Platelet Aggregation : Activated platelets express glycoprotein IIb/IIIa receptors that bind fibrinogen, linking platelets together and forming a temporary "platelet plug" to prevent blood loss.

Secondary Hemostasis

This stage stabilizes the platelet plug through the formation of a fibrin mesh, which is achieved via a cascade of enzymatic reactions involving clotting factors. It consists of two main pathways that converge into a common pathway:

Extrinsic Pathway
- Initiated by tissue factor (TF) released from damaged tissues, which activates factor VII to VIIa.
- The TF-VIIa complex then activates factor X to Xa in the presence of calcium ions.

Intrinsic Pathway
- Triggered by exposure of blood to subendothelial collagen, activating factor XII.
- This pathway involves several factors (XII, XI, IX, and VIII) leading to the activation of factor X.

Common Pathway

- Both pathways converge at factor Xa, which combines with factor Va and calcium ions to form the prothrombinase complex.
- This complex converts prothrombin (factor II) into thrombin (factor IIa).
- Thrombin then cleaves fibrinogen (factor I) into fibrin (factor Ia), forming long strands that weave through the platelet plug.
- Finally, thrombin activates factor XIII, which cross-links fibrin strands to stabilize the clot.

Here's a tabular representation of the blood clotting factors:

Factor Number	Name	Alternate Name	Primary Role in Clotting
I	Fibrinogen	-	Converts to fibrin to form the clot mesh.
II	Prothrombin	-	Converts to thrombin, activating fibrin.
III	Tissue Factor	Thromboplastin	Initiates the extrinsic pathway.
IV	Calcium	Ca^{2+}	Essential for all pathways of clotting.
V	Proaccelerin	Labile Factor	Cofactor for Factor X in thrombin activation.
VI	-	No longer recognized	-
VII	Proconvertin	Stable Factor	Activates Factor X in the extrinsic pathway.
VIII	Anti-Hemophilic Factor A	-	Cofactor for Factor IX in the intrinsic pathway.
IX	Christmas Factor	Anti-Hemophilic Factor B	Activates Factor X in the intrinsic pathway.
X	Stuart-Prower Factor	-	Converts prothrombin to thrombin.
XI	Plasma Thromboplastin Antecedent	-	Activates Factor IX in the intrinsic pathway.
XII	Hageman Factor	-	Initiates the intrinsic pathway.
XIII	Fibrin-Stabilizing Factor	-	Stabilizes the fibrin clot.

This table summarizes the factors, their names, and their roles in the clotting process.

(6.5) Anticoagulants

Anticoagulants, commonly referred to as blood thinners, are medications that prevent blood clotting by interfering with the normal coagulation processes. They are essential in managing conditions that pose a risk of thromboembolism, such as deep vein thrombosis (DVT), pulmonary embolism (PE), and atrial fibrillation. Here's an overview of the types of anticoagulants, their mechanisms of action, and their clinical applications.

Types of Anticoagulants

1. Unfractionated Heparin (UFH)

- Mechanism : Activates antithrombin III, which inhibits thrombin and factor Xa, thereby preventing the conversion of fibrinogen to fibrin.

- Administration : Typically administered intravenously.

- Monitoring : Requires regular monitoring using activated partial thromboplastin time (aPTT).

- Use : Often used in acute settings due to its rapid onset and short half-life.

2. Low Molecular Weight Heparins (LMWH)

- Examples : Enoxaparin, dalteparin, tinzaparin.

- Mechanism : Similar to UFH but with a more predictable anticoagulant response; primarily inhibit factor Xa.

- Administration : Given subcutaneously.

- Monitoring : Routine monitoring is generally not required, except in specific cases like renal impairment or pregnancy.

3. Vitamin K Antagonists (VKAs)

- Example : Warfarin.

- Mechanism : Inhibits vitamin K epoxide reductase, affecting the synthesis of vitamin K-dependent clotting factors (II, VII, IX, X) and proteins C and S.

- Monitoring : Requires regular monitoring via International Normalized Ratio (INR).

- Use : Long-term management of thromboembolic disorders.

4. Direct Thrombin Inhibitors

- Examples : Bivalirudin, argatroban, dabigatran.

- Mechanism : Directly inhibit thrombin's ability to convert fibrinogen to fibrin.

- Administration : Can be given intravenously or orally (e.g., dabigatran).

- Use : Useful in patients with heparin-induced thrombocytopenia or those requiring anticoagulation during procedures.

5. Direct Factor Xa Inhibitors

- Examples : Rivaroxaban, apixaban, edoxaban.

- Mechanism: Directly inhibit factor Xa, preventing the conversion of prothrombin to thrombin.

- Administration : Orally administered.

- Use : Increasingly used for DVT and PE treatment and prevention.

Mechanism of Action

Anticoagulants work through various mechanisms:

- **Inhibition of Coagulation Factors :** Many anticoagulants target specific coagulation factors within the intrinsic or extrinsic pathways of the coagulation cascade. For instance, heparins enhance the activity of antithrombin III to inhibit thrombin and factor Xa.

- **Direct Inhibition :** Direct thrombin inhibitors and direct factor Xa inhibitors block specific enzymes in the coagulation cascade without requiring antithrombin.

- **Vitamin K Antagonism :** VKAs disrupt the synthesis of vitamin K-dependent clotting factors by inhibiting their formation in the liver.

Clinical Applications

Anticoagulants are prescribed for various conditions including:

- Prevention and treatment of venous thromboembolism (DVT/PE).

- Management of atrial fibrillation to reduce stroke risk.

- Treatment of certain types of heart attacks and unstable angina.

- Prevention of clot formation during surgical procedures.

HOW BLOOD CLOTS

① NORMAL BLOOD VESSEL → ② INJURED BLOOD VESSEL → ③ PLATELET PLUG FORMATION → ④ FORMED PLUG CLOT

(6.6) Physiological basis of blood groups

Physiological Basis of Blood Groups

Blood groups are classifications of blood based on the presence or absence of specific antigens on the surface of red blood cells (RBCs) and corresponding antibodies in the plasma. The most recognized blood group systems are the **ABO** and **Rh** systems, which are crucial for blood transfusion compatibility.

ABO Blood Group System

The ABO blood group system consists of four main types: **A**, **B**, **AB**, and **O**. This classification is determined by the presence of two primary antigens, A and B, on the RBC surface:

- Group A : Contains antigen A and produces anti-B antibodies.
- Group B : Contains antigen B and produces anti-A antibodies.
- Group AB : Contains both antigens A and B, with no antibodies against either.
- Group O : Lacks both antigens A and B, but produces both anti-A and anti-B antibodies.

The inheritance of these blood types is governed by alleles from both parents. The A and B alleles are codominant, meaning that if an individual inherits one of each, they will express both antigens (blood type AB). The O allele is recessive, resulting in no antigen expression when paired with either A or B alleles.

Blood Groups in the ABO System

Blood Group	Antigens on RBC's	Antibodies in Plasma	Can Receive From	Can Donate To
A	A	Anti - B	A, O	A, AB
B	B	Anti - A	B, O	B, AB
AB	A and B	None	A,B,AB,O (Universal Acceptor)	AB
O	None	Anti A and Anti B	O	A,B,AB,O (Universal Donor)

Rh Blood Group System

The Rh system is another significant classification, primarily defined by the presence of the RhD antigen. Individuals who have this antigen are classified as Rh-positive (+), while those who do not are Rh-negative

(–). The Rh system includes several other antigens (e.g., C, c, E, e), but RhD is the most clinically relevant due to its implications in pregnancy and transfusions.

Immune Response to Blood Groups

The immune system plays a critical role in blood group physiology. Each individual develops antibodies against the blood group antigens they lack. For example, a person with type A blood will have performed anti-B antibodies that can cause agglutination (clumping) if exposed to type B blood. This immune response is particularly important during transfusions; mismatched blood types can lead to severe reactions or even death.

Genetic Basis

The genetic basis for these blood groups lies in specific genes that encode glycosyltransferases responsible for adding sugar molecules to precursor substances on the RBC membrane. The A allele encodes an enzyme that adds N-acetyl galactosamine to the H antigen, forming antigen A. The B allele adds D-galactose to form antigen B. The O allele does not produce a functional enzyme, resulting in no additional sugars being added.

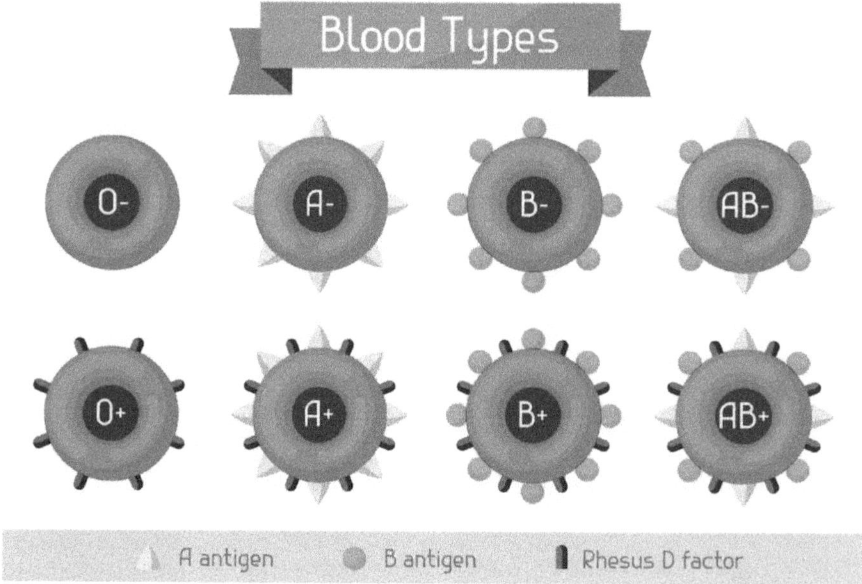

Physiological basis of plasma proteins

- **Albumin :** The most abundant plasma protein, crucial for maintaining blood's osmotic pressure and transporting various substances throughout the body.
- **Globulins :** Includes different types such as alpha, beta, and gamma globulins, which are involved in immune defence and transport functions.

- **Fibrinogen :** A key protein in the clotting process, converting to fibrin to form blood clots.
- **Regulatory Proteins :** Include enzymes and other proteins that regulate various physiological processes.

These proteins are primarily synthesized in the liver and play vital roles in maintaining homeostasis, supporting immune function, and facilitating blood coagulation. Abnormal levels can indicate various health issues such as liver disease or inflammation.

Plasma Protein	Normal Level	Percentage of Total Plasma Proteins	Primary Functions
Albumin	3.5–5.0 g/dL	55%	Maintains osmotic pressure, transports hormones and drugs
Globulins	2.0–2.5 g/dL	38%	Immune response, transport of ions, hormones, and lipids
Fibrinogen	0.2–0.45 g/dL	7%	Essential for blood clotting
Regulatory Proteins	<1%	<1%	Regulation of gene expression and enzyme activity
Clotting Factors	<1%	<1%	Conversion of fibrinogen into fibrin during coagulation

(6.7) Introduction to Anemia and Jaundice

Anemia and jaundice are two medical conditions that can often be interrelated, both affecting the blood and overall health. Understanding their physiological basis, causes, symptoms, and implications is crucial for diagnosis and treatment.

Anemia

Definition : Anemia is a condition characterized by a deficiency in healthy red blood cells (RBCs) or hemoglobin, which impairs the blood's ability to carry oxygen to the body's tissues.

Causes :

- **Nutritional Deficiencies :** Iron deficiency is the most common cause, but deficiencies in vitamin B12, folate, and other nutrients can also lead to anemia.
- **Blood Loss :** This can occur due to heavy menstruation, gastrointestinal bleeding, or trauma.
- **Bone Marrow Disorders :** Conditions like aplastic anemia affect the production of RBCs in the bone marrow.
- **Hemolysis :** Increased destruction of RBCs can occur in conditions such as sickle cell disease or autoimmune disorders.

Symptoms :

- Common symptoms include fatigue, weakness, pale skin, shortness of breath, dizziness, and cold extremities.
- Severe cases may lead to chest pain, rapid heartbeat, and cognitive issues due to insufficient oxygen delivery.

Jaundice

Definition : Jaundice is a condition that results in yellowing of the skin and eyes due to elevated levels of bilirubin in the blood. Bilirubin is a by-product of the breakdown of hemoglobin from old RBCs.

Causes :
- Liver Dysfunction : Conditions like hepatitis or cirrhosis can impair bilirubin processing.
- Hemolytic Anemia: Increased breakdown of RBCs leads to excess bilirubin production.
- Bile Duct Obstruction : Gallstones or tumors can block bile flow, causing bilirubin accumulation.

Symptoms :
- The primary symptom is yellowing of the skin and sclera (the whites of the eyes).
- Other symptoms may include dark urine, pale stools, itching, and abdominal pain depending on the underlying cause.

Interrelationship

Anemia and jaundice can coexist; for example, hemolytic anemia leads to increased RBC breakdown, resulting in both anemia (due to decreased RBC count) and jaundice (due to elevated bilirubin levels). Understanding these conditions is essential for effective diagnosis and treatment strategies. If either condition is suspected, medical evaluation is crucial for determining the underlying causes and appropriate interventions.

Chapter – 7

(7.1) Classification of immunity: Innate, acquired and Artificial

Classification of Immunity

Immunity can be broadly classified into three categories: Innate immunity, acquired immunity, and artificial immunity. Each type plays a crucial role in the body's defence against pathogens.

Innate Immunity

Innate immunity, also known as natural or non-specific immunity, is the body's first line of defence against pathogens. It is characterized by:

- Immediate Response : Innate immunity acts quickly, often within hours of pathogen exposure.
- Non-Specific Mechanisms : This type does not differentiate between specific pathogens; it responds to general features of pathogens.

- **Components :**
  - Physical Barriers : Skin and mucous membranes prevent pathogen entry.
  - Chemical Barriers : Substances like lysozyme and stomach acid help neutralize pathogens.
  - Cellular Components : Includes phagocytic cells (e.g., macrophages, neutrophils) and natural killer cells that engulf and destroy invaders.
  - Humoral Factors : Complement proteins and cytokines play roles in inflammation and pathogen destruction.

Acquired Immunity

Acquired immunity, also referred to as adaptive immunity, develops after exposure to specific pathogens. It is characterized by:

- Specific Response : Acquired immunity targets specific pathogens with precision.
- Memory Formation : This type of immunity can "remember" past infections, allowing for a quicker response upon re-exposure.

Acquired immunity can be further divided into two subtypes:

1. Active Immunity :

- Developed through natural infection or vaccination.
- Involves the production of antibodies by the immune system.
- Long-lasting, sometimes lifelong.

2. Passive Immunity :
- Involves the transfer of antibodies from another source (e.g., maternal antibodies during pregnancy).
- Provides immediate but short-term protection, lasting only weeks to months.

Artificial Immunity

Artificial immunity is a subset of acquired immunity that is induced through deliberate actions, such as vaccination. This can be categorized into:

- Artificial Active Immunity : Achieved through vaccination, where a weakened or inactive form of a pathogen is introduced to stimulate an immune response.
- Artificial Passive Immunity : Involves the administration of preformed antibodies (e.g., immune globulin) to provide immediate protection against specific diseases.

Summary Table of Immunity Types

Type of Immunity	**Characteristics**	**Duration**
Innate Immunity	Non – Specific, immediate response	Present at birth
Acquired Immunity	Specific, involves memory	Develops over time
Article Immunity	Induced through vaccines or antibody transfer	Varies bases on type

(7.2) Mechanisms Involved in Immunity: Humoral and T-Cell Mediated Immunity

The immune system employs various mechanisms to protect the body from pathogens. Two primary types of adaptive immunity are humoral immunity, which is mediated by B cells, and cell-mediated immunity, which is primarily driven by T cells. Each mechanism has distinct functions and processes.

Humoral Immunity (B-Cell Mediated)

Humoral immunity involves the production of antibodies by B lymphocytes (B cells) and is crucial for defending against extracellular pathogens such as bacteria and viruses. Key features include:

- B Cell Activation : When B cells encounter specific antigens, they bind to these antigens through their B-cell receptors. This binding triggers their activation, often requiring help from helper T cells that release cytokines to stimulate B cell proliferation and differentiation.

- Antibody Production : Activated B cells differentiate into plasma cells, which are responsible for producing antibodies (immunoglobulins). These antibodies can neutralize pathogens directly or mark them for destruction by other immune cells.

- Memory Cells : Some activated B cells become memory cells, which persist long-term in the body. These cells enable a faster and more robust response upon re-exposure to the same antigen, forming the basis for immunological memory and vaccine effectiveness.

- Mechanisms of Action :

  - Neutralization : Antibodies can neutralize toxins or block pathogen entry into host cells.
  - Opsonization : Antibodies coat pathogens, making them more recognizable to phagocytes.
  - Complement Activation : Antibodies can activate the complement system, leading to pathogen lysis and inflammation.

T-Cell Mediated Immunity

T-cell mediated immunity involves T lymphocytes (T cells) and is essential for targeting infected or abnormal cells, including those infected by viruses and some cancerous cells. Key components include:

- Types of T Cells :

  - Helper T Cells (CD4+ T Cells): These cells assist in activating B cells and cytotoxic T cells by releasing cytokines. They play a vital role in orchestrating the immune response.

- Cytotoxic T Cells (CD8+ T Cells) : These cells directly kill infected or cancerous cells by recognizing specific antigens presented on major histocompatibility complex (MHC) molecules on the surface of these target cells.

- Activation Process : T cells require antigen presentation by professional antigen-presenting cells (APCs), such as dendritic cells or macrophages. Upon recognition of the antigen-MHC complex, T cells undergo clonal expansion and differentiation into effector and memory T cells.

- Mechanisms of Action :

- Direct Killing : Cytotoxic T cells induce apoptosis in infected or malignant cells through the release of perforins and granzymes.

- Cytokine Release : Helper T cells produce cytokines that enhance the activity of other immune components, including B cells and macrophages.

Mechanism	**Key Players**	**Main Functions**
Humoral Immunity	B Cells	Antibody production, neutralization, opsonization
T-Cell Mediated Immunity	T Cells	Direct killing of infected/cancerous cells, cytokine signalling

(7.3) Hypersensitivity

Hypersensitivity reactions are exaggerated immune responses that can lead to tissue damage and various clinical manifestations. They are classified into four main types according to the Gell and Coombs classification system: Type I, Type II, Type III, and Type IV. Each type involves different immune mechanisms and mediators.

Type I Hypersensitivity (Immediate Hypersensitivity)

- **Mechanism :** This reaction is primarily mediated by Immunoglobulin E (IgE) antibodies. Upon exposure to an allergen, IgE binds to mast cells and basophils, leading to their degranulation and the release of inflammatory mediators such as histamine, leukotrienes, and cytokines.

- **Clinical Manifestations :** Symptoms can range from mild allergic reactions (e.g., hay fever, urticaria) to severe anaphylaxis, which is a life-threatening systemic response.

- **Examples :** Allergic rhinitis, asthma, food allergies, and insect sting allergies.

Type II Hypersensitivity (Cytotoxic Hypersensitivity)

- **Mechanism :** In this type, IgG or IgM antibodies bind to antigens on the surface of cells. This binding activates the complement system or recruits immune cells (like natural killer cells) that mediate cell destruction.

- **Clinical Manifestations :** This can result in conditions such as hemolytic anemia, where red blood cells are destroyed, or autoimmune diseases where the body attacks its own tissues.
- **Examples**: Hemolytic disease of the newborn, Goodpasture syndrome, and certain drug reactions.

Type III Hypersensitivity (Immune Complex-Mediated Hypersensitivity)

- **Mechanism :** This reaction involves the formation of immune complexes between antigens and antibodies (IgG or IgM). These complexes can deposit in tissues and activate the complement system, leading to inflammation and tissue damage.

- **Clinical Manifestations :** The effects can be systemic or localized depending on where the immune complexes accumulate.

- **Examples :** Serum sickness, systemic lupus erythematosus (SLE), rheumatoid arthritis, and vasculitis.

Type IV Hypersensitivity (Delayed-Type Hypersensitivity)

- **Mechanism :** Unlike the other types, this reaction is mediated by T cells rather than antibodies. Upon re-exposure to an antigen, sensitized T cells release cytokines that recruit macrophages and other inflammatory cells to the site of exposure.

- **Clinical Manifestations :** Symptoms typically develop 24 to 72 hours after exposure to the allergen.

- **Examples :** Contact dermatitis (e.g., poison ivy), tuberculin skin test reactions, and graft-versus-host disease.

Summary Table of Hypersensitivity Types

Type	Mediators	Mechanism	Examples
Type I	IgE	Immediate reaction; mast cell degranulation	Allergic rhinitis, anaphylaxis
Type II	IgG or IgM	Antibody-mediated cell destruction	Hemolytic anemia, Goodpasture syndrome
Type III	IgG or IgM	Immune complex deposition	Serum sickness, systemic lupus erythematosus
Type IV	T cells	Delayed cellular response	Contact dermatitis, tuberculin reaction

Chapter – 8

(8.1)Functional anatomy of cardiovascular system

Functional Anatomy of the Cardiovascular System

The cardiovascular system, also known as the circulatory system, is a complex network responsible for transporting blood, nutrients, gases, hormones, and waste products throughout the body. Its primary components include the heart, blood vessels, and blood. Understanding the functional anatomy of this system is crucial for comprehending how it maintains homeostasis and supports bodily functions.

Heart

The heart is a muscular organ located in the thoracic cavity, between the lungs. It functions as the central pump of the cardiovascular system.

- **Chambers :** The heart consists of four chambers:
  - **Right Atrium :** Receives deoxygenated blood from the body via the superior and inferior venacavae.
  - **Right Ventricle :** Pumps deoxygenated blood to the lungs through the pulmonary artery for oxygenation.
  - **Left Atrium :** Receives oxygenated blood from the lungs via the pulmonary veins.
  - **Left Ventricle :** Pumps oxygenated blood to the rest of the body through the aorta.

- **Valves :** The heart contains four main valves that ensure unidirectional blood flow:
  - **Tricuspid Valve :** Located between the right atrium and right ventricle.
  - **Pulmonary Valve :** Between the right ventricle and pulmonary artery.
  - **Mitral (Bicuspid) Valve :** Between the left atrium and left ventricle.
  - **Aortic Valve :** Between the left ventricle and aorta.

- **Septum :** The heart is divided into right and left sides by a muscular wall called the septum, which prevents mixing of oxygenated and deoxygenated blood.

Blood Vessels

Blood vessels form a network that transports blood throughout the body. They can be classified into three main types:

- **Arteries :** Carry oxygen-rich blood away from the heart (except for pulmonary arteries). They have thick, elastic walls to withstand high pressure.

- **Veins :** Return deoxygenated blood to the heart (except for pulmonary veins). They have thinner walls than arteries and contain valves to prevent backflow due to lower pressure.

- **Capillaries :** Microscopic vessels that connect arteries and veins. Their thin walls allow for efficient exchange of gases, nutrients, and waste products between blood and tissues.

Blood

Blood is a specialized connective tissue composed of various components:

- **Red Blood Cells (Erythrocytes) :** Transport oxygen from the lungs to tissues and carbon dioxide from tissues back to the lungs.

- **White Blood Cells (Leukocytes) :** Part of the immune system; they help defend against infections.

- **Platelets (Thrombocytes) :** Involved in blood clotting to prevent excessive bleeding.

- **Plasma :** The liquid component of blood that carries cells, nutrients, hormones, proteins, and waste products.

Circulatory Pathways

The cardiovascular system operates through two primary circulatory pathways:

1. Systemic Circulation :
- Oxygenated blood is pumped from the left ventricle into the aorta.
- Blood travels through systemic arteries to deliver oxygen and nutrients to tissues.
- Deoxygenated blood returns to the right atrium via systemic veins.

2. Pulmonary Circulation :
- Deoxygenated blood is pumped from the right ventricle into the pulmonary artery.
- Blood travels to the lungs for gas exchange (oxygenation).
- Oxygenated blood returns to the left atrium via pulmonary veins.

(8.2) Cardiac Cycle

The cardiac cycle refers to the sequence of events that occur during one complete heartbeat, encompassing the contraction and relaxation of the heart chambers. It is crucial for understanding how the heart functions to pump blood effectively throughout the body. The cardiac cycle can be divided into several phases, primarily categorized into systole (contraction) and diastole (relaxation).

Phases of the Cardiac Cycle

1. Atrial Systole

- **Description :** The atria contract, pushing blood into the ventricles.
- **Mechanism :** The sinoatrial (SA) node generates an electrical impulse that spreads through the atria, causing them to contract.
- **Valves :** The atrioventricular (AV) valves (tricuspid and mitral) are open, allowing blood flow from the atria to the ventricles.

2. Ventricular Systole

- **Isovolumetric Contraction :**
  - **Description :** The ventricles begin to contract, increasing pressure within them.
  - **Mechanism :** All heart valves are closed at this stage, preventing blood from entering or leaving the ventricles.

- **Ventricular Ejection :**
  - **Description :** Once ventricular pressure exceeds that in the aorta and pulmonary artery, the semilunar valves (aortic and pulmonary) open.
  - **Result :** Blood is ejected from the ventricles into the systemic circulation (from the left ventricle) and pulmonary circulation (from the right ventricle).

3. Isovolumetric Relaxation

- **Description :** After ventricular contraction, the ventricles relax.
- **Mechanism :** The semilunar valves close as ventricular pressure falls below arterial pressure, preventing backflow of blood.
- **Valves :** All valves are closed during this phase; no blood enters or leaves the ventricles.

4. Ventricular Filling

- **Early Diastole :**
  - **Description :** As ventricular pressure continues to drop, the AV valves open when ventricular pressure falls below atrial pressure.
  - **Result :** Blood flows passively from the atria into the ventricles.
- **Late Diastole (Atrial Systole) :**

- Description : The atria contract again, completing ventricular filling by pushing additional blood into the ventricles.

Phase	Description	Key Events
Atrial Systole	Atria contract; blood moves into ventricles	AV valves open
Ventricular Systole	Ventricles contract; blood ejected into arteries	Isovolumetric contraction followed by ejection
Isovolumetric Relaxation	Ventricles relax; all valves closed	No change in volume; pressure drops
Ventricular Filling	Blood flows from atria to ventricles	AV valves open; passive filling followed by atrial contraction

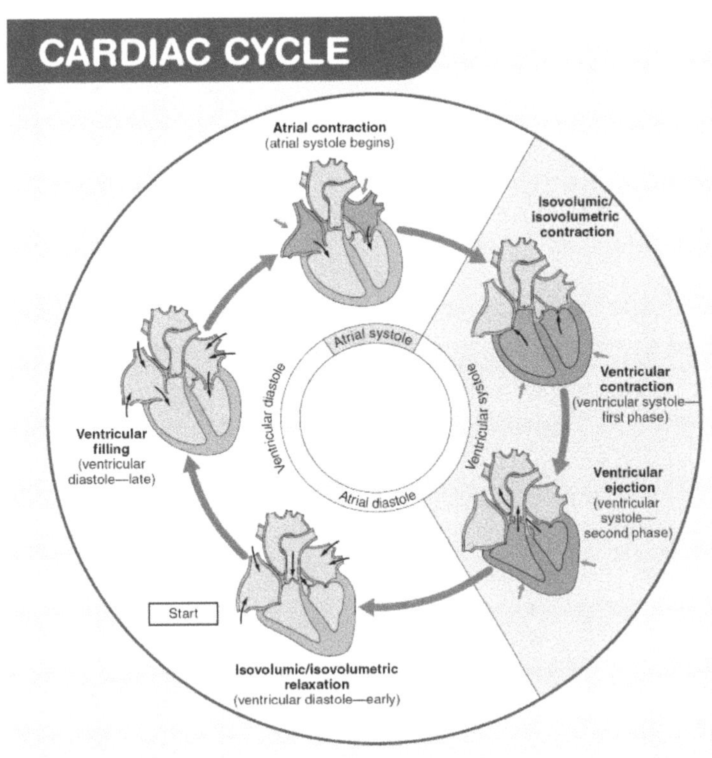

(8.3) Heart Sound

Heart sounds are the noises produced by the heart during the cardiac cycle, primarily resulting from the closure of heart valves. These sounds are crucial for assessing cardiac function and can provide valuable information about heart health. The two primary heart sounds are S1 and S2, with additional sounds (S3 and S4) sometimes present in certain conditions.

Primary Heart Sounds

1. First Heart Sound (S1)

- Description : Often referred to as "lub," S1 marks the beginning of ventricular systole.
- Cause : It is produced by the closure of the atrioventricular (AV) valves (tricuspid and mitral valves) as the ventricles contract.
- Timing : S1 occurs just after the onset of ventricular contraction when the pressure in the ventricles exceeds that in the atria.

2. Second Heart Sound (S2)

- **Description :** Known as "dub," S2 signifies the end of ventricular systole.
- **Cause :** It results from the closure of the semilunar valves (aortic and pulmonary valves) when ventricular pressure falls below arterial pressure.
- **Timing :** S2 occurs at the end of ventricular contraction, just before the ventricles begin to relax.

Additional Heart Sounds

3. Third Heart Sound (S3)

- **Description :** Often described as a "ventricular gallop," S3 is a low-frequency sound that occurs shortly after S2.
- **Cause :** It is associated with rapid ventricular filling during early diastole when blood rushes into a compliant ventricle.
- **Clinical Significance :** While it can be normal in children and young adults, an S3 sound in older adults may indicate heart failure or volume overload.

4. Fourth Heart Sound (S4)

- **Description :** Known as an "atrial gallop," S4 occurs just before S1.
- **Cause :** It results from atrial contraction and is associated with a stiff or hypertrophied ventricle that resists filling.
- **Clinical Significance :** An S4 sound is often indicative of conditions such as hypertension, aortic stenosis, or ischemic heart disease.

Summary Table of Heart Sounds

Heart Sound	Description	Cause	Clinical Significance
S1	"Lub"	Closure of AV valves	Normal finding; indicates start of systole
S2	"Dub"	Closure of semilunar valves	Normal finding; indicates end of systole
S3	"Ventricular gallop"	Rapid ventricular filling	May indicate heart failure in older adults
S4	"Atrial gallop"	Atrial contraction against stiff ventricle	Often indicates hypertrophy or stiffness

Auscultation

Heart sounds are typically assessed using a stethoscope during a physical examination. The points on the chest where heart sounds are best heard include:

- Aortic Area : Right second intercostal space (S2 prominent).
- Pulmonic Area : Left second intercostal space.
- Tricuspid Area : Lower left sternal border (S1 prominent).
- Mitral Area : Fifth intercostal space at the midclavicular line (S1 prominent).

(8.4) Regulation of cardiac output and venous return

Cardiac output (CO) and venous return are critical components of the cardiovascular system, ensuring adequate blood flow to meet the metabolic demands of the body. Their regulation involves complex interactions between various physiological mechanisms.

Regulation of Cardiac Output

Cardiac output is defined as the volume of blood pumped by the heart per minute and is calculated using the formula:

CO = HR \times SV

where "HR" is heart rate and "SV" is stroke volume. The regulation of cardiac output is influenced by several factors:

1. Heart Rate (HR) :

- **Intrinsic Regulation :** The sinoatrial (SA) node generates electrical impulses that set the heart rate, typically between 60 to 100 beats per minute.
- **Autonomic Nervous System :**
  - Sympathetic Stimulation : Increases heart rate through catecholamines (e.g., epinephrine), enhancing chronotropy (rate of contraction).
  - Parasympathetic Stimulation : Reduces heart rate via acetylcholine, primarily affecting resting conditions.

2. Stroke Volume (SV) :

- Preload : Refers to the degree of stretch of the cardiac muscle fibres at the end of diastole. Increased venous return raises preload, enhancing stroke volume through the Frank-Starling mechanism.
- Contractility : The inherent strength of cardiac muscle contraction, influenced by factors such as catecholamines and thyroid hormones. Increased contractility leads to greater stroke volume.
- Afterload : The resistance the ventricles must overcome to eject blood. Higher systemic vascular resistance decreases stroke volume, while lower resistance facilitates ejection.

3. Hormonal Influences :

- Hormones such as adrenaline and norepinephrine enhance both heart rate and contractility.
- Thyroid hormones can also increase cardiac output by enhancing metabolic activity.

Regulation of Venous Return

Venous return is the amount of blood returning to the heart and is crucial for maintaining cardiac output. Several factors influence venous return:

1. Pressure Gradient : The difference in pressure between the peripheral veins and the right atrium drives venous return. Increased pressure in the veins or decreased pressure in the right atrium enhances return flow.

2. Venous Tone : The state of constriction or dilation of veins affects their capacity to hold blood. Sympathetic stimulation causes venous constriction, increasing venous return.

3. Muscle Pump Mechanism : Skeletal muscle contractions during physical activity compress veins, pushing blood toward the heart.

4. Respiratory Pump : During inhalation, intrathoracic pressure decreases, facilitating increased venous return from the abdominal cavity to the thoracic cavity.

5. Blood Volume : Increased blood volume from fluid retention or transfusion raises venous return, while decreased volume from haemorrhage reduces it.

Interaction Between Cardiac Output and Venous Return

The relationship between cardiac output and venous return is integral to maintaining hemodynamic stability:

- An increase in venous return leads to increased preload, which enhances stroke volume according to the Frank-Starling law.
- Conversely, if cardiac output exceeds venous return (e.g., during intense exercise), it can lead to a decrease in filling pressures and potentially compromise perfusion.

(8.5) Physiological basis of ECG

The electrocardiogram (ECG or EKG) is a vital tool in cardiology that provides insights into the electrical activity of the heart. Understanding the physiological basis of the ECG involves exploring how electrical impulses are generated and propagated through the heart, leading to coordinated contractions.

Cardiac Electrical Activity

1. Pacemaker Cells :
- The heart's rhythm is primarily controlled by specialized pacemaker cells located in the sinoatrial (SA) node. These cells have the unique ability to spontaneously depolarize, generating electrical impulses without external stimuli. This process occurs due to the gradual influx of sodium ions, leading to a threshold potential that triggers an action potential.

2. Action Potential Propagation :
- Once initiated by the SA node, the electrical impulse spreads through the atria, causing atrial depolarization (represented by the P wave on the ECG). The impulse then reaches the atrioventricular (AV) node, where it is briefly delayed to allow for complete atrial contraction before passing into the ventricles via the bundle of His and Purkinje fibers.

3. Ventricular Depolarization :
- The QRS complex on the ECG represents ventricular depolarization. This phase involves rapid depolarization of the ventricles, leading to their contraction. The QRS complex is characterized by a sharp upward deflection (R wave) followed by downward deflections (Q and S waves), reflecting the sequential activation of different ventricular regions.

4. Repolarization :
- After depolarization, the ventricles undergo repolarization, which is represented by the T wave on the ECG. This phase restores the resting membrane potential of cardiac cells, allowing them to prepare for the next cycle of depolarization.

ECG Waveforms

- P Wave : Indicates atrial depolarization.
- PR Interval : The time from the beginning of atrial depolarization to the beginning of ventricular depolarization.
- QRS Complex : Reflects ventricular depolarization.
- T Wave : Represents ventricular repolarization.

Clinical Significance

The ECG provides valuable information regarding heart rate, rhythm, and any potential abnormalities in electrical conduction or myocardial ischemia. Variations in waveforms can indicate various cardiac conditions:

- Arrhythmias : Changes in rhythm can be diagnosed by analysing intervals and wave shapes.
- Ischemia or Infarction : ST-segment changes can indicate myocardial ischemia or infarction.
- Electrolyte Imbalances : Alterations in T wave morphology can suggest electrolyte disturbances.

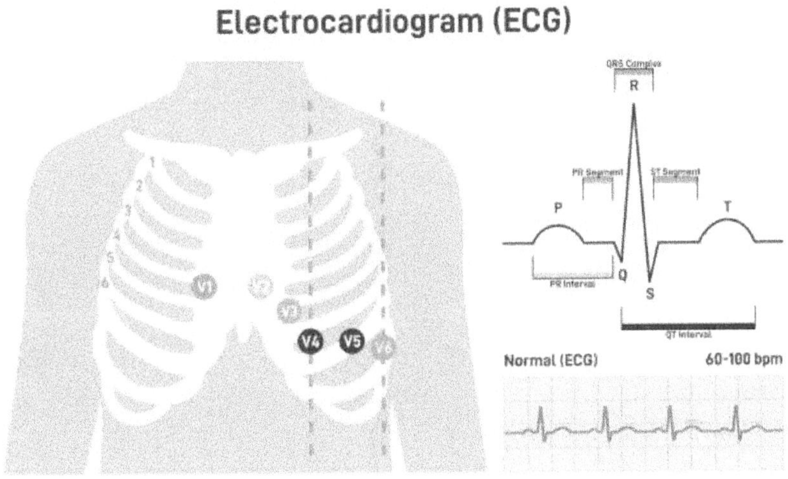

Electrocardiogram (ECG)

(8.6) Heart-rate and its regulation & Arterial Pulse

Heart Rate and Its Regulation

Heart rate (HR) refers to the number of times the heart beats per minute and is a crucial parameter for assessing cardiovascular health. The normal resting heart rate for adults typically ranges from 60 to 100 beats per minute. Heart rate can vary significantly based on physiological demands, emotional states, and various external factors.

Factors Influencing Heart Rate

1. Intrinsic Factors :

- Sinoatrial (SA) Node : The SA node, located in the right atrium, is the primary pacemaker of the heart. It generates electrical impulses that initiate each heartbeat. The intrinsic firing rate of the SA node is approximately 60 to 100 beats per minute.

- Autonomic Nervous System : The autonomic nervous system (ANS) plays a significant role in regulating heart rate through its two branches:

- Sympathetic Nervous System : Increases heart rate through the release of catecholamines (e.g., norepinephrine). Sympathetic stimulation enhances the firing rate of the SA node and increases myocardial contractility.

- Parasympathetic Nervous System : Decreases heart rate via the vagus nerve, which releases acetylcholine. This action slows down the firing rate of the SA node.

2. Hormonal Influences :

- Hormones such as epinephrine and norepinephrine released from the adrenal medulla during stress or physical activity can increase heart rate.
- Thyroid hormones can also enhance heart rate by increasing metabolic activity in cardiac tissues.

3. Physiological Factors :

- Exercise : Physical activity increases metabolic demand, leading to an increase in heart rate to supply more oxygen and nutrients to working muscles.
- Body Temperature : Elevated body temperature can increase heart rate, while lower temperatures may decrease it.
- Age and Gender : Resting heart rates tend to be higher in children and can vary between genders, with women often having slightly higher rates than men.

4. Pathological Conditions :

- Conditions such as fever, anaemia, hyperthyroidism, or heart diseases can lead to abnormal increases (tachycardia) or decreases (bradycardia) in heart rate.

Measurement of Heart Rate

Heart rate can be measured using various methods:

- Pulse Palpation : Feeling the pulse at specific locations (e.g., wrist, neck).
- Electrocardiogram (ECG) : Provides a continuous recording of electrical activity and allows for precise measurement of heart rate.
- Heart Rate Monitors : Wearable devices that use sensors to track heart rate continuously during activities.

Arterial Pulse

The arterial pulse is the rhythmic expansion and contraction of an artery as blood is pumped through it with each heartbeat. It serves as a vital indicator of cardiovascular health and can provide valuable information about heart rate, rhythm, and the condition of the arterial system.

Characteristics of Arterial Pulse

1. Pulse Wave : The pulse wave is generated by the force of blood ejected from the heart during ventricular systole. This wave travels through the arterial system, causing the arteries to expand and contract.

2. Palpable Pulse Points : The pulse can be felt at various locations on the body where arteries are close to the skin surface. Common pulse points include:
- Radial Pulse : Located at the wrist, on the thumb side.
- Carotid Pulse : Found in the neck, beside the trachea.
- Femoral Pulse : Located in the groin area.
- Popliteal Pulse : Found behind the knee.
- Dorsalis Pedis Pulse : Located on the top of the foot.

3. Pulse Rate : The number of beats felt per minute, which typically correlates with heart rate. A normal resting pulse rate for adults ranges from 60 to 100 beats per minute.

4. Pulse Rhythm : The regularity of pulse beats can indicate whether heart rhythms are normal (regular) or irregular (arrhythmias).

5. Pulse Quality : The strength and character of the pulse can vary:
- Strong/Bounding : Indicates increased stroke volume or decreased vascular resistance.

- Weak/Thready : May suggest low blood volume or decreased cardiac output.
- Absent : Indicates potential vascular occlusion or severe circulatory issues.

Clinical Significance

1. Assessment of Cardiovascular Health :

- The arterial pulse provides insights into heart function and circulatory status. Changes in pulse characteristics can indicate underlying health issues.

2. Monitoring Conditions :

- Conditions such as hypertension, peripheral artery disease, and heart failure can be assessed through pulse examination.

3. Detection of Arrhythmias :

- Irregularities in pulse rhythm can signal arrhythmias or other cardiac conditions that may require further investigation.

4. Evaluation of Peripheral Circulation :

- Assessing pulses in extremities helps evaluate blood flow and detect conditions like peripheral artery disease or thrombosis.

Measurement Techniques

- **Palpation :** The most common method involves using fingers to feel for a pulse at specific sites.
- **Doppler Ultrasound :** A non-invasive technique that uses sound waves to assess blood flow and measure pulse in areas difficult to palpate.
- **Pulse Oximetry :** A device that measures oxygen saturation levels in blood but also provides heart rate information based on pulse detection.

(8.7) Systemic arterial blood pressure and its control

Systemic Arterial Blood Pressure and Its Control

Systemic arterial blood pressure is the force exerted by circulating blood on the walls of the arteries. It is a critical measure of cardiovascular health and is essential for ensuring adequate perfusion of tissues and organs. Blood pressure is typically expressed as two values: systolic pressure (the pressure during heartbeats) and diastolic pressure (the pressure between heartbeats).

Components of Blood Pressure

1. Systolic Blood Pressure (SBP) :

- The maximum pressure in the arteries during ventricular contraction (systole).
- Normal values are generally around 90 to 120 mmHg.

2. Diastolic Blood Pressure (DBP) :

- The minimum pressure in the arteries during ventricular relaxation (diastole).
- Normal values are typically around 60 to 80 mmHg.

3. Mean Arterial Pressure (MAP) :

- An average blood pressure in a person's arteries during one cardiac cycle, calculated as:
- MAP is an important indicator of perfusion to vital organs.

Regulation of Blood Pressure

The regulation of systemic arterial blood pressure involves multiple mechanisms that work together to maintain homeostasis:

1. Neural Regulation :

- **Autonomic Nervous System :**
  - The sympathetic nervous system increases heart rate and contractility, leading to increased cardiac output and vasoconstriction, which raises blood pressure.
  - The parasympathetic nervous system decreases heart rate, contributing to lower blood pressure.
  - Baroreceptors : Located in the carotid sinus and aortic arch, these stretch receptors detect changes in blood pressure. Increased blood pressure stimulates baroreceptors, which send signals to the central nervous system to decrease heart rate and promote vasodilation. Conversely, decreased blood pressure leads to increased heart rate and vasoconstriction.

2. Hormonal Regulation :

- Renin-Angiotensin-Aldosterone System (RAAS) :

- Renin is released by the kidneys in response to low blood flow or low sodium levels, leading to the production of angiotensin II, which causes vasoconstriction and stimulates aldosterone release from the adrenal glands. Aldosterone promotes sodium and water retention, increasing blood volume and pressure.

- Antidiuretic Hormone (ADH) : Released from the posterior pituitary gland in response to high plasma osmolality or low blood volume, ADH promotes water reabsorption in the kidneys, increasing blood volume and pressure.

- Natriuretic Peptides : Released by the heart in response to increased atrial stretch due to high blood volume, these hormones promote vasodilation and increase renal excretion of sodium and water, lowering blood pressure.

3. Local Regulation :

- Autoregulation : Tissues can regulate their own blood flow through local mechanisms that respond to changes in metabolic activity (e.g., increased carbon dioxide or decreased oxygen levels lead to vasodilation).
- Endothelial Factors : The endothelium releases substances such as nitric oxide (a vasodilator) and endothelin (a vasoconstrictor) that influence vascular tone.

Factors Affecting Blood Pressure

1. Cardiac Output : Increased cardiac output raises blood pressure.
2. Blood Volume : Higher blood volume increases venous return and cardiac output, thus raising blood pressure.
3. Vascular Resistance : Increased resistance in peripheral vessels due to vasoconstriction raises blood pressure.
4. Viscosity of Blood : Higher viscosity increases resistance, contributing to higher blood pressure.

Chapter – 9

(9.1) Comparison of physiology of skeletal muscles, cardiac muscles and smooth muscles

Comparison of the Physiology of Skeletal, Cardiac, and Smooth Muscles

Skeletal, cardiac, and smooth muscles are the three primary types of muscle tissue in the human body, each with distinct structures, functions, and physiological characteristics. This comparison highlights their differences and similarities.

1. Structural Characteristics

1. Structural Characteristics

Feature	Skeletal Muscle	Cardiac Muscle	Smooth Muscle
Cell Shape	Long, cylindrical fibers	Branched, striated fibers	Spindle-shaped fibers
Striations	Striated (striped appearance)	Striated (less pronounced)	Non-striated (smooth appearance)
Nuclei	Multinucleated (nuclei at periphery)	Uninucleated (central nucleus)	Uninucleated (central nucleus)
Control	Voluntary control	Involuntary control	Involuntary control
Intercalated Discs	Absent	Present (specialized junctions)	Absent

2. Functional Characteristics

2. Functional Characteristics

Feature	Skeletal Muscle	Cardiac Muscle	Smooth Muscle
Contraction Speed	Fast	Moderate to fast	Slow
Fatigue Resistance	Moderate	High (due to rich blood supply)	High (can sustain contractions for long periods)
Energy Source	Primarily anaerobic and aerobic	Primarily aerobic	Primarily aerobic
Regulation of Contraction	Neural input from somatic nervous system	Autonomic nervous system and hormones	Autonomic nervous system, hormones, and local factors

3. Mechanism of Contraction

- **Skeletal Muscle :**
  - Contraction is initiated by action potentials from motor neurons at the neuromuscular junction.
  - Calcium ions released from the sarcoplasmic reticulum bind to troponin, leading to the sliding filament mechanism where actin and myosin filaments interact to produce contraction.
- **Cardiac Muscle :**
  - Contraction is initiated by intrinsic electrical activity generated by pacemaker cells in the sinoatrial (SA) node.
  - Calcium ions enter from both extracellular sources and the sarcoplasmic reticulum, binding to troponin similarly to skeletal muscle, leading to contraction.
- **Smooth Muscle :**
  - Contraction can be triggered by various stimuli including hormones, neurotransmitters, or mechanical stretch.
  - Calcium binds to calmodulin instead of troponin. The calcium-calmodulin complex activates myosin light chain kinase, which phosphorylates myosin and initiates contraction.

4. Role in the Body

- **Skeletal Muscle :**
  - Responsible for voluntary movements, posture maintenance, and heat production through muscle contractions.
- **Cardiac Muscle :**
  - Responsible for involuntary contractions that pump blood throughout the body; it maintains a rhythmic heartbeat.
- **Smooth Muscle :**
  - Found in walls of hollow organs (e.g., intestines, blood vessels); it regulates involuntary movements such as peristalsis and vascular tone.

(9.2) Physiology of Muscle Contraction

Muscle contraction is a complex physiological process that enables movement and various bodily functions. This process varies among the three types of muscle tissue: skeletal, cardiac, and smooth muscles. Below is a detailed overview of the mechanisms involved in muscle contraction for each type.

1. Skeletal Muscle Contraction

Mechanism :

- **Neuromuscular Junction Activation :** The process begins when an action potential travels down a motor neuron to the neuromuscular junction, releasing the neurotransmitter acetylcholine (ACh) into the synaptic cleft.

- **Depolarization :** ACh binds to receptors on the muscle fiber's sarcolemma, causing depolarization and the generation of an action potential that spreads along the sarcolemma and into the T-tubules.

- **Calcium Release :** The action potential triggers the sarcoplasmic reticulum to release calcium ions (Ca^{2+}) into the cytoplasm.

- **Cross-Bridge Formation :** Calcium binds to troponin, causing a conformational change that moves tropomyosin away from binding sites on actin filaments. Myosin heads then attach to these exposed sites, forming cross-bridges.

- **Sliding Filament Mechanism :** ATP binds to myosin heads, breaking the cross-bridge. ATP hydrolysis repositions the myosin heads, allowing them to bind to new actin sites. This cycle of attachment, pivoting, and detachment pulls actin filaments toward the center of the sarcomere, resulting in muscle shortening (sarcomere shortening) and contraction.

2. Cardiac Muscle Contraction

Mechanism :

- **Intrinsic Regulation :** Cardiac muscle contraction is initiated by pacemaker cells in the sinoatrial (SA) node, which generate action potentials autonomously.
- **Propagation of Action Potentials :** These impulses spread through the atria and reach the atrioventricular (AV) node, then propagate through the bundle of His and Purkinje fibers, causing coordinated contraction.
- **Calcium-Induced Calcium Release :** Similar to skeletal muscle, calcium ions play a crucial role. When action potentials reach cardiac muscle fibers, Ca^{2+} enters from extracellular fluid through voltage-gated calcium channels. This influx triggers further release of Ca^{2+} from the sarcoplasmic reticulum.

- **Cross-Bridge Cycling :** The mechanism of contraction is similar to that in skeletal muscle; calcium binds to troponin, exposing binding sites on actin for myosin heads. ATP hydrolysis allows for cross-bridge cycling and muscle contraction.

3. Smooth Muscle Contraction

Mechanism :

- **Stimulus Initiation :** Smooth muscle contraction can be triggered by various stimuli, including hormones, neurotransmitters, or mechanical stretch. Unlike skeletal muscle, smooth muscle does not require direct neural stimulation for every contraction.
- **Calcium Binding :** When stimulated, calcium ions enter the cell and are released from the sarcoplasmic reticulum. Calcium binds to calmodulin rather than troponin.
- **Activation of Myosin Light Chain Kinase (MLCK) :** The calcium-calmodulin complex activates MLCK, which phosphorylates myosin light chains. This phosphorylation increases myosin ATPase activity.
- **Cross-Bridge Formation and Sliding Mechanism :** Phosphorylated myosin interacts with actin filaments to form cross-bridges. The sliding mechanism occurs as myosin heads pull on actin filaments, resulting in contraction.
- **Relaxation :** Smooth muscle relaxation occurs when calcium levels decrease, allowing myosin phosphatase to dephosphorylate myosin light chains and reduce contractile activity.

Summary of Muscle Contraction Mechanisms

Muscle Type	Initiation of Contraction	Calcium Source	Cross-Bridge Formation	Relaxation Mechanism
Skeletal Muscle	Action potential from motor neuron	Released from sarcoplasmic reticulum	Myosin heads bind to actin after calcium binds to troponin	Calcium pumped back into SR; tropomyosin covers binding sites
Cardiac Muscle	Pacemaker cells generate action potentials	Extracellular fluid and sarcoplasmic reticulum	Myosin heads bind to actin after calcium binds to troponin	Calcium levels decrease; relaxation occurs
Smooth Muscle	Hormonal or mechanical stimuli	Extracellular fluid and sarcoplasmic reticulum	Myosin heads bind after calcium binds to calmodulin	Decrease in calcium; myosin phosphatase dephosphorylates myosin

(10.1) Lipoproteins - VLDL, LDL and HDL Triglycerides

Lipoproteins: VLDL, LDL, HDL, and Triglycerides

Lipoproteins are complex particles that transport lipids (fats) in the bloodstream, including cholesterol and triglycerides. They play crucial roles in lipid metabolism and cardiovascular health. This overview focuses on the main types of lipoproteins—very low-density lipoproteins (VLDL), low-density lipoproteins (LDL), and high-density lipoproteins (HDL)—as well as triglycerides, their functions, and their implications for health.

1. Types of Lipoproteins

Very Low-Density Lipoproteins (VLDL)

- **Composition :** VLDL contains a high proportion of triglycerides (approximately 60-70%) and some cholesterol.
- **Function :** VLDL is produced by the liver and is responsible for transporting triglycerides from the liver to peripheral tissues. It plays a role in delivering energy to cells.
- **Metabolism :** VLDL is converted into intermediate-density lipoprotein (IDL) as triglycerides are hydrolysed by lipoprotein lipase, eventually leading to the formation of LDL.

Low-Density Lipoproteins (LDL)

- **Composition :** LDL is rich in cholesterol (about 50% cholesterol) and contains less triglyceride compared to VLDL.
- **Function :** Often referred to as "bad cholesterol," LDL carries cholesterol from the liver to cells throughout the body. High levels of LDL can lead to plaque build-up in arteries, increasing the risk of atherosclerosis and cardiovascular disease.
- **Clinical Significance :** Elevated LDL levels are associated with an increased risk of heart disease. Monitoring LDL levels is crucial for assessing cardiovascular health.

High-Density Lipoproteins (HDL)

- **Composition :** HDL contains a higher proportion of protein (approximately 50% protein) and less cholesterol.
- **Function :** Known as "good cholesterol," HDL is involved in reverse cholesterol transport, where it collects excess cholesterol from peripheral tissues and transports it back to the liver for excretion or recycling.
- **Clinical Significance :** Higher levels of HDL are associated with a lower risk of heart disease. HDL helps protect against atherosclerosis by removing excess cholesterol from the bloodstream.

2. Triglycerides

- **Definition :** Triglycerides are the most common type of fat found in the body. They consist of three fatty acid chains linked to a glycerol molecule.
- **Function :** Triglycerides serve as a major energy source for the body. They are stored in adipose tissue and released into the bloodstream when energy is needed.
- **Metabolism :** After eating, dietary fats are broken down into fatty acids and reassembled into triglycerides. These are then packaged into chylomicrons for transport through the lymphatic system into the bloodstream.
- **Clinical Significance :** Normal triglyceride levels are under 150 mg/dL. Elevated levels can increase the risk of pancreatitis and cardiovascular diseases, independent of other lipid levels.

3. Interactions Between Lipoproteins and Triglycerides

- Triglyceride-rich lipoproteins (TRLs), such as chylomicrons and VLDL, play significant roles in lipid transport and metabolism. They deliver triglycerides to tissues for energy use or storage.
- The metabolism of TRLs involves complex interactions with HDL and LDL:
- Cholesterol Ester Transfer Protein (CETP) facilitates the transfer of triglycerides from VLDL to HDL, enriching HDL with triglycerides while depleting VLDL of triglycerides.
- The remnants of TRLs after triglyceride hydrolysis can contribute to LDL formation.

(10.2) Functions of skin, sweat glands and sebaceous glands

Functions of Skin, Sweat Glands, and Sebaceous Glands

The skin is the largest organ of the body and plays a vital role in maintaining overall health. It is composed of multiple layers and contains various structures, including sweat glands and sebaceous glands, each contributing to its diverse functions.

Functions of Skin

1. Protective Barrier :
- The skin serves as the first line of defence against pathogens, physical injuries, and harmful substances. It prevents the entry of bacteria and viruses while protecting against mechanical damage and UV radiation.

2. Temperature Regulation :
- The skin helps regulate body temperature through mechanisms such as sweating and vasodilation or vasoconstriction of blood vessels. When the body heats up, sweat glands produce sweat that evaporates, cooling the surface of the skin.

3. Sensation :
- The skin contains numerous sensory receptors that detect touch, pressure, temperature, and pain. This sensory information is transmitted to the brain, allowing for appropriate responses to environmental stimuli.

4. Immune Defense :
- Skin plays a crucial role in the immune system by producing antimicrobial substances and housing immune cells that help detect and combat infections.

5. Vitamin D Production :
- When exposed to sunlight, the skin synthesizes vitamin D, which is essential for calcium absorption and bone health.

6. Water Barrier :
- The skin prevents excessive water loss through its barrier function, helping maintain hydration levels in the body.

Functions of Sweat Glands

Sweat glands are specialized structures within the skin that produce sweat. They play several key roles:

1. Thermoregulation :
- The primary function of sweat glands is to help regulate body temperature. When body temperature rises, sweat is secreted onto the skin surface, where it evaporates, dissipating heat.

2. Excretion :
- Sweat glands also aid in excreting waste products such as urea, salts, and toxins from the body through perspiration.

3. Hydration Maintenance :
- By controlling moisture levels on the skin's surface, sweat glands contribute to maintaining skin hydration and preventing dryness.

Functions of Sebaceous Glands

Sebaceous glands are associated with hair follicles and secrete an oily substance known as sebum. Their functions include:

1. Lubrication :
- Sebum produced by sebaceous glands helps keep the skin and hair moisturized and prevents them from becoming dry or brittle.

2. Protection :
- Sebum forms a protective barrier on the skin's surface that helps prevent water loss and shields against environmental factors such as bacteria and fungi.

3. Antimicrobial Properties :
- Sebum contains antimicrobial compounds that can inhibit the growth of harmful microorganisms on the skin.

4. Thermoregulation Support :
- By providing a lipid layer on the skin's surface, sebum can help enhance the effectiveness of sweat evaporation for temperature regulation.

Chapter – 11

(11.1) Ovulation

Ovulation is a critical physiological process in the menstrual cycle, marked by the release of a mature egg from the ovary. This event is essential for reproduction, as it allows for the possibility of fertilization by sperm. Here's a detailed description of ovulation, its timing, hormonal regulation, and implications for fertility.

Definition and Timing

- **Definition :** Ovulation refers to the rupture of the dominant follicle in the ovary, leading to the release of a secondary oocyte into the abdominal cavity. The oocyte is then captured by the fimbriae of the fallopian tube, where it may become fertilized by sperm.

- **Timing :** Ovulation typically occurs around the midpoint of the menstrual cycle, approximately 14 days before the onset of menstruation. In a standard 28-day cycle, this places ovulation around days 13 to 15, although this can vary among individuals and cycles.

Hormonal Regulation

Ovulation is regulated by a complex interplay of hormones:

1. Follicle-Stimulating Hormone (FSH) :

- FSH is released from the anterior pituitary gland and stimulates the growth and maturation of ovarian follicles during the follicular phase of the menstrual cycle. Several follicles begin to develop, but usually only one becomes dominant.

2. Luteinizing Hormone (LH) :

- A surge in LH levels triggers ovulation. This surge occurs approximately 24 to 36 hours before the egg is released and is stimulated by rising estrogen levels produced by the developing follicles.

3. Estrogen :

- As follicles mature, they produce increasing amounts of estrogen, which prepares the endometrium for potential implantation and also contributes to the LH surge that induces ovulation.

The Ovulation Process

1. Follicular Development :

- During the first half of the menstrual cycle (follicular phase), several follicles grow under FSH stimulation. Typically, only one follicle becomes dominant and matures fully.

2. LH Surge :

- Just before ovulation, high levels of estrogen lead to a surge in LH levels. This surge causes enzymatic changes that weaken the follicular wall.

3. Rupture and Release :

- The dominant follicle ruptures, releasing the secondary oocyte into the peritoneal cavity through a structure known as the stigma. The fimbriae of the fallopian tube then capture the released oocyte.

4. Post-Ovulation :

- After ovulation, if fertilization occurs, the fertilized egg travels down to implant in the uterus. If not fertilized, the oocyte disintegrates within 12-24 hours, leading to menstruation as hormone levels drop.

Fertility Considerations

- The ovulatory phase represents a window of fertility; sperm can survive in the female reproductive tract for up to five days, while an egg remains viable for about 12-24 hours after ovulation . Tracking ovulation can help individuals trying to conceive or those using natural family planning methods.

FROM OVULATION TO IMPLANTATION

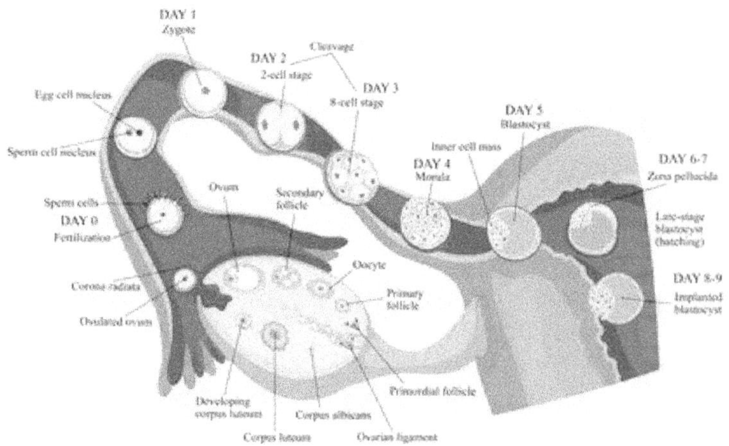

(11.2) Spermatogenesis

Spermatogenesis is the biological process through which male gametes, known as spermatozoa or sperm cells, are produced in the male reproductive system. This intricate process occurs primarily in the seminiferous tubules of the testes and involves several stages that transform undifferentiated germ cells into mature sperm.

Overview of Spermatogenesis

1. Location : Spermatogenesis takes place in the seminiferous tubules of the testes, where spermatogonia (the precursor germ cells) reside.

2. Duration : The entire process from spermatogonia to mature spermatozoa typically takes about 64 to 72 days.

3. Hormonal Regulation : The process is regulated by hormones, including:
- **Follicle-Stimulating Hormone (FSH) :** Stimulates spermatogenesis and supports Sertoli cells.
- **Luteinizing Hormone (LH) :** Stimulates Leydig cells to produce testosterone, which is crucial for the maturation of sperm.
- **Testosterone :** Promotes the development and maintenance of male reproductive tissues and sperm production.

Stages of Spermatogenesis

Spermatogenesis can be divided into three main stages:

1. Spermato-cytogenesis :
- This initial stage involves the mitotic division of spermatogonia.
- Types of Spermatogonia :
  - Type A Spermatogonia : These replenish the stem cell population.
  - Type B Spermatogonia : These differentiate into primary spermatocytes.
- Each primary spermatocyte is diploid (2n) and undergoes meiosis.

2. Meiosis :
- The primary spermatocytes undergo two meiotic divisions:
  - Meiosis I : Each primary spermatocyte divides to form two secondary spermatocytes, which are haploid (n).
  - Meiosis II : Each secondary spermatocyte divides to produce two spermatids, resulting in a total of four haploid spermatids from one primary spermatocyte.

3. Spermiogenesis :
- This final stage involves the transformation of round spermatids into elongated, motile spermatozoa.
- Key changes during this phase include:

- Development of a tail (flagellum) for motility.
- Formation of the acrosome at the head, which contains enzymes necessary for fertilization.
- Loss of excess cytoplasm to streamline the sperm structure.

Maturation and Storage

After spermiogenesis, the mature spermatozoa are transported to the epididymis, where they undergo further maturation and are stored until ejaculation. During this time, they gain motility and are prepared for potential fertilization.

Factors Affecting Spermatogenesis

Spermatogenesis can be influenced by various factors, including:

- **Hormonal Levels :** Fluctuations in FSH, LH, and testosterone can impact sperm production.
- **Temperature :** The testes must be maintained at a temperature slightly lower than body temperature for optimal sperm production.
- **Lifestyle Factors :** Diet, alcohol consumption, drug use, and exposure to environmental toxins can adversely affect spermatogenesis.
- **Age :** Sperm production may decline with age, potentially leading to infertility.

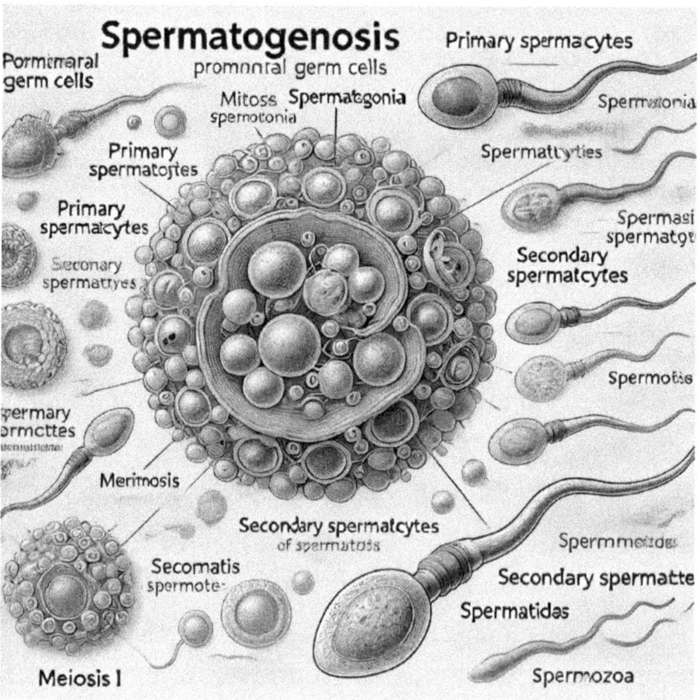

(11.3) Oogenesis

Oogenesis is the biological process through which female gametes, or ova, are formed in the ovaries. This complex and highly regulated process begins before birth and continues throughout a woman's reproductive life. Here's a detailed overview of oogenesis, including its stages and significance.

Definition of Oogenesis

Oogenesis is the process of developing female gametes from primordial germ cells. It involves several stages that lead to the formation of mature ova, ready for potential fertilization.

Stages of Oogenesis

Oogenesis can be divided into distinct phases:

1. Multiplication Phase (Proliferative Phase) :

- Timing : This phase occurs during fatal development.
- Process : Primordial germ cells in the ovaries undergo mitotic divisions to form numerous oogonia (the precursor cells). Some of these oogonia will develop into primary oocytes.

2. Growth Phase :

- Development : The oogonia that transform into primary oocytes begin to grow and accumulate cytoplasmic components necessary for future development.
- Arrest in Meiosis : Primary oocytes enter meiosis but are arrested in prophase I. This arrest can last for years, often until puberty.

3. Maturation Phase :

- Activation at Puberty : With the onset of puberty, hormonal changes trigger the activation of some primary oocytes each menstrual cycle.
- Meiosis Resumption : The activated primary oocyte completes meiosis I, resulting in a secondary oocyte and a polar body (which typically degenerates).
- Meiosis II Arrest : The secondary oocyte begins meiosis II but arrests at metaphase II until fertilization occurs.

4. Ovulation Phase :

- Triggered by a surge in luteinizing hormone (LH), ovulation leads to the release of the mature secondary oocyte from the Graafian follicle into the fallopian tube.
- If fertilization occurs, meiosis II is completed, yielding a mature ovum and another polar body. If fertilization does not occur, the secondary oocyte degenerates.

Significance of Oogenesis

- Reproductive Success : Oogenesis is critical for female fertility as it ensures the production of healthy and genetically diverse ova necessary for sexual reproduction.

- Hormonal Regulation : The process is intricately regulated by hormones such as FSH (Follicle-Stimulating Hormone) and LH (Luteinizing Hormone), which control follicular development and ovulation.

- Potential Implications : Disorders or abnormalities in oogenesis can lead to infertility, miscarriages, or genetic disorders, highlighting the importance of understanding this process.

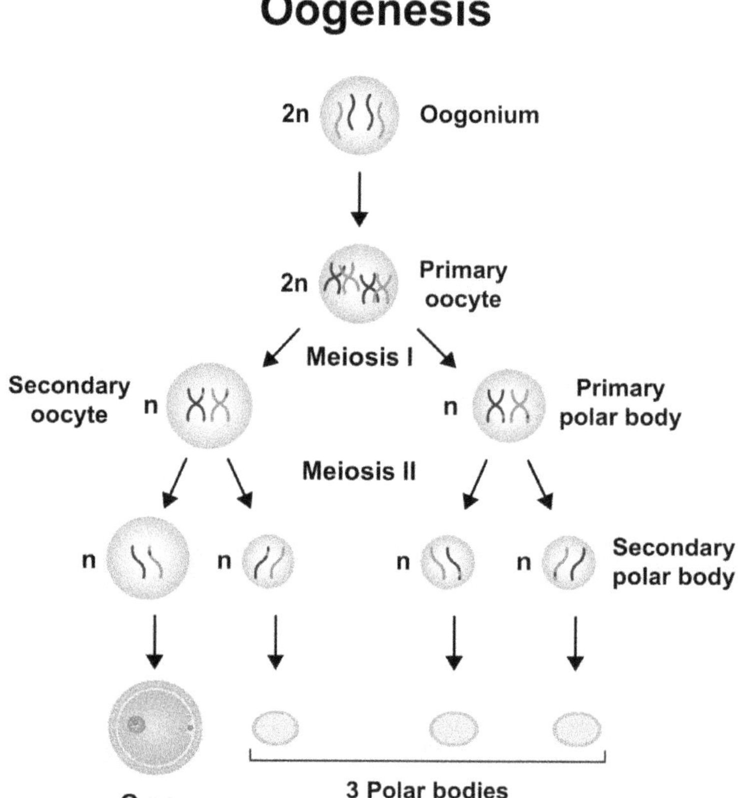

(11.4) Menstrual Cycle

The menstrual cycle is a complex physiological process that prepares the female body for potential pregnancy each month. It consists of four main phases: menstruation, the follicular phase, ovulation, and the luteal phase. Understanding these phases helps in recognizing fertility patterns and overall reproductive health.

Phases of the Menstrual Cycle

1. Menstrual Phase :

- Duration : Typically lasts 3 to 7 days.
- Description : This phase marks the shedding of the uterine lining (endometrium) when a fertilized egg does not implant. It begins on the first day of menstruation, which is considered Day 1 of the cycle.
- Hormonal Changes : A drop in estrogen and progesterone levels triggers this shedding. Common symptoms during this phase may include cramps, bloating, and mood changes.

2. Follicular Phase :

- Duration : Lasts about 13 to 14 days, starting on Day 1 of menstruation and continuing until ovulation.
- Description : During this phase, the pituitary gland releases Follicle-Stimulating Hormone (FSH), stimulating the growth of ovarian follicles. Usually, one follicle becomes dominant and matures into an egg.
- Hormonal Changes : Estrogen levels rise as the follicles develop, leading to thickening of the uterine lining in preparation for a possible pregnancy.

3. Ovulation :

- Timing : Occurs approximately midway through the cycle, around Day 14 in a typical 28-day cycle.
- Description : A mature egg is released from the dominant follicle in the ovary and enters the fallopian tube.
- Hormonal Changes : A surge in Luteinizing Hormone (LH) triggers ovulation. This is the most fertile period, and unprotected intercourse during this time can lead to conception.

4. Luteal Phase :

- Duration : Lasts about 14 days, from ovulation until the start of the next menstrual period.
- Description : After ovulation, the ruptured follicle transforms into the corpus luteum, which secretes progesterone to maintain the uterine lining.
- Hormonal Changes : If fertilization occurs, progesterone supports pregnancy by maintaining the uterine lining. If not fertilized, hormone levels drop, leading to menstruation as the uterine lining sheds.

Summary of Menstrual Cycle

Phase	Duration	Key Events	Hormonal Changes
Menstrual Phase	3-7 days	Shedding of uterine lining	Decreased estrogen and progesterone
Follicular Phase	13-14 days	Follicle maturation; uterine lining thickens	Increased estrogen due to follicle growth
Ovulation	1 day	Release of mature egg	Surge in LH; peak in estrogen
Luteal Phase	~14 days	Corpus luteum formation; preparation for pregnancy	Increased progesterone; decreased estrogen if no pregnancy occurs

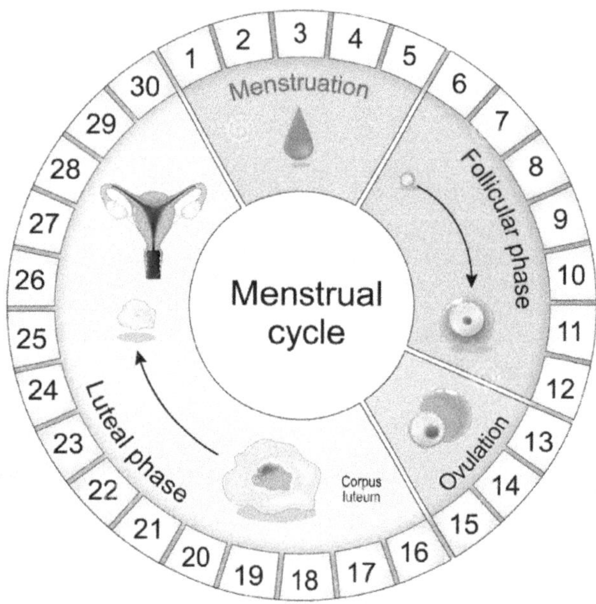

Chapter – 12

(12.1) Functional anatomy of urinary tract

The urinary tract is a vital system in the human body responsible for the formation, storage, and elimination of urine. Its functional anatomy includes several key components, each with specific roles in maintaining homeostasis and eliminating waste products. Below is a detailed overview of the functional anatomy of the urinary tract.

Components of the Urinary Tract

1. Kidneys

- **Location :** The kidneys are two bean-shaped organs located in the retroperitoneal space, positioned below the ribs towards the middle of the back.
- **Function :**
- **Filtration :** The primary role of the kidneys is to filter blood to remove waste products and excess substances, producing urine.
- **Regulation :** They help regulate blood pressure, electrolyte balance, acid-base balance, and fluid homeostasis.
- **Hormone Production :** The kidneys secrete hormones such as erythropoietin (which stimulates red blood cell production) and renin (which regulates blood pressure).

2. Ureters

- **Structure :** Two narrow tubes (approximately 22-30 cm long) that transport urine from the kidneys to the bladder.
- **Function :**
- **Peristalsis :** Muscular walls of the ureters contract rhythmically to propel urine downward from the renal pelvis to the bladder.
- **Prevention of Reflux :** The ureters enter the bladder at an oblique angle, which helps prevent backflow (vesicoureteral reflux) during bladder contraction.

3. Bladder

- **Structure :** A hollow, muscular organ located in the lower abdomen that serves as a reservoir for urine.
- **Capacity :** The bladder can typically hold about 400-600 mL of urine.
- **Function :**
- **Storage :** It stores urine until it is convenient to void.
- **Detrusor Muscle :** The bladder walls contain smooth muscle (detrusor muscle) that contracts to expel urine during urination.
- **Trigone Area :** A triangular region at the base of the bladder that includes openings for the ureters and urethra.

4. Urethra

- **Structure :** A tube that connects the bladder to the external environment, allowing for urine excretion.
- **Length and Functionality :**
- In males, it is longer (approximately 20 cm) and also serves as a passage for semen.
- In females, it is shorter (approximately 4 cm) and solely functions for urine excretion.
- **Sphincter Muscles :**
- The internal urethral sphincter (smooth muscle) is under involuntary control, while the external urethral sphincter (skeletal muscle) is under voluntary control, allowing for conscious regulation of urination.

Functional Mechanisms

- Urine Formation :

- Urine formation begins in the kidneys through three processes:

1. Filtration : Blood plasma is filtered in the glomeruli within nephrons, forming filtrate that will become urine.

2. Reabsorption : Essential substances such as water, glucose, and electrolytes are reabsorbed back into the bloodstream from the renal tubules.

3. Secretion : Additional waste products and excess ions are secreted into the tubular fluid.

- Storage and Elimination :
- As urine fills the bladder, stretch receptors signal to the brain when it reaches capacity.
- Upon appropriate signals from the nervous system, detrusor muscle contraction occurs while sphincters relax to allow for urination.

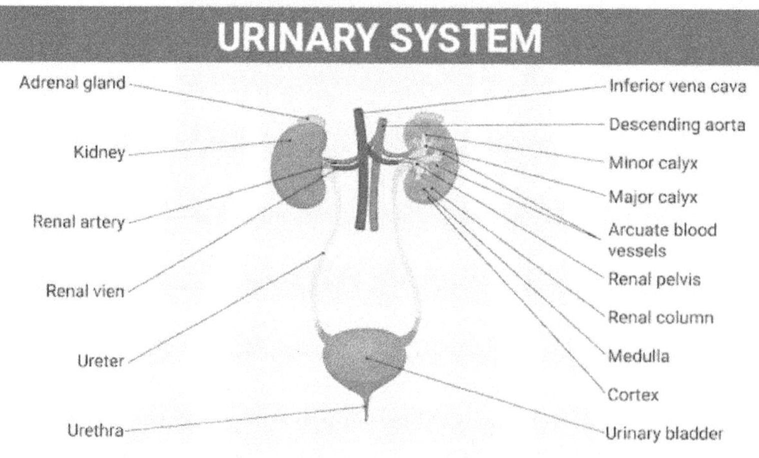

(12.2) Functions of kidney

The kidneys are essential organs with multiple critical functions that contribute to overall health and homeostasis. Here's an overview of the primary functions of the kidneys based on the provided information.

Major Functions of the Kidneys

1. Waste Filtration and Excretion :

- The kidneys filter waste products and excess substances from the blood, including urea, creatinine, and toxins. This filtration process occurs in the nephrons, the functional units of the kidneys, where blood is filtered through structures called glomeruli. The resulting filtrate is processed to form urine, which is excreted from the body.

2. Regulation of Fluid and Electrolyte Balance :

- The kidneys maintain the body's fluid balance by regulating the volume of water and electrolytes (such as sodium, potassium, and calcium) in the blood. They adjust the reabsorption of these substances based on the body's needs, ensuring that homeostasis is maintained.

3. Acid-Base Balance :

- The kidneys help regulate blood pH by excreting hydrogen ions and generating bicarbonate, which buffers acidity in the blood. This function is crucial for maintaining a stable internal environment.

4. Blood Pressure Regulation :

- The kidneys play a vital role in regulating blood pressure through the renin-angiotensin-aldosterone system (RAAS). They release renin in response to low blood pressure or low sodium levels, leading to a cascade of events that ultimately increases blood pressure.

5. Hormone Production :

- The kidneys produce several important hormones:
  - Erythropoietin : Stimulates red blood cell production in the bone marrow in response to low oxygen levels in the blood.
  - Renin : Involved in blood pressure regulation.
  - Active Vitamin D : The kidneys convert inactive vitamin D into its active form (calcitriol), which is essential for calcium absorption and bone health.

6. Regulation of Blood Volume :

- By adjusting the amount of water reabsorbed during urine formation, the kidneys play a crucial role in regulating overall blood volume, which affects blood pressure.

Summary

The kidneys are vital organs that perform multiple essential functions:

- Waste Filtration : Removing waste products from the blood.

- Fluid and Electrolyte Balance : Regulating water and electrolyte levels.

- Acid-Base Balance : Maintaining pH levels in the blood.

- Blood Pressure Regulation : Contributing to overall cardiovascular health.

- Hormone Production : Producing erythropoietin, renin, and active vitamin D.

- Blood Volume Regulation : Influencing overall fluid balance in the body.

These functions highlight the importance of kidney health for maintaining homeostasis and preventing various health issues. Regular monitoring and care are essential for those with kidney-related conditions or risk factors.

(12.3) Mechanism of formation of urine, Control of micturition

Mechanism of Formation of Urine

Urine formation is a vital process carried out by the kidneys, primarily occurring in the nephrons. This process involves several key steps: glomerular filtration, selective reabsorption, tubular secretion, and concentration of urine. Here's a detailed overview of each step:

1. Glomerular Filtration

- **Process :** Blood enters the glomerulus through the afferent arteriole. The glomerulus is a network of capillaries surrounded by Bowman's capsule. Due to the narrower diameter of the efferent arteriole compared to the afferent arteriole, blood pressure builds up in the glomerulus, facilitating filtration.
- **Filtration Membrane :** The filtration occurs through a specialized membrane that allows water and small solutes (e.g., glucose, amino acids, urea) to pass while retaining larger molecules like proteins and blood cells.
- **Filtrate :** The fluid that enters Bowman's capsule is called glomerular filtrate or nephric filtrate, which is initially composed of water, electrolytes, nutrients, and waste products.

2. Selective Reabsorption

- **Location :** This process primarily occurs in the proximal convoluted tubule (PCT) but also takes place in other parts of the nephron, including the loop of Henle and distal convoluted tubule (DCT).
- **Mechanism :** Approximately 99% of the filtrate is reabsorbed back into the bloodstream. This involves:
- **Active Transport :** Nutrients such as glucose and amino acids are actively transported back into the peritubular capillaries.
- **Passive Transport :** Water follows solutes osmotically; around 75% of water is reabsorbed in the PCT.
- **Electrolyte Reabsorption :** Sodium ions are reabsorbed actively, while chloride ions follow passively.

3. Tubular Secretion

- **Process :** This occurs mainly in the distal convoluted tubule and collecting ducts. It involves the active transport of substances from the blood into the tubular fluid.
- **Substances Secreted :** Waste products such as urea, uric acid, creatinine, excess ions (e.g., potassium and hydrogen ions), and certain drugs are secreted into the nephron to be excreted in urine.
- **Purpose :** This step helps regulate blood pH and eliminate additional waste products that were not filtered during glomerular filtration.

4. Concentration of Urine

- **Mechanism :** The concentration of urine occurs primarily in the loop of Henle and collecting ducts:
  - In the loop of Henle, water is reabsorbed from the filtrate into the surrounding hyperosmotic interstitial fluid, concentrating the urine.
  - In the presence of antidiuretic hormone (ADH), more water is reabsorbed in the collecting ducts, leading to more concentrated urine. In contrast, absence of ADH results in dilute urine.

Summary of Urine Formation Steps

Step	Description
Glomerular Filtration	Blood is filtered in the glomerulus; water and small solutes enter Bowman's capsule as filtrate.
Selective Reabsorption	Essential nutrients and water are reabsorbed into blood from renal tubules.
Tubular Secretion	Waste products and excess ions are secreted from blood into renal tubules.
Concentration of Urine	Water reabsorption occurs in response to ADH; urine concentration is adjusted based on hydration status.

Control of Micturition

Micturition, or urination, is the process by which urine is expelled from the bladder. It involves both voluntary and involuntary mechanisms:

1. Neural Control

- **Stretch Receptors :** As urine fills the bladder, stretch receptors in its walls send signals to the spinal cord and brain when a certain threshold is reached (typically around 300-400 mL).

- **Reflex Arc :** The micturition reflex involves a spinal reflex that triggers contraction of the detrusor muscle (the bladder muscle) while relaxing the internal urethral sphincter.

2. Voluntary Control

- **Cerebral Cortex Involvement :** The brain allows for voluntary control over urination through conscious decision-making to either initiate or delay micturition.

- **External Urethral Sphincter :** This skeletal muscle can be contracted voluntarily to prevent urination until an appropriate time.

3. Phases of Micturition

1. Filling Phase :

- The bladder gradually fills with urine while detrusor muscle remains relaxed due to sympathetic nervous system activity.

2. Voiding Phase :

- When ready to urinate, signals from stretch receptors lead to increased parasympathetic activity causing detrusor contraction and sphincter relaxation.

3. Post-Micturition :

- After voiding, bladder pressure decreases, and sphincters return to their resting state.

(12.4) Formation of faeces and mechanism of defecation

Formation of Faeces and Mechanism of Defecation

The formation of faeces is a crucial process in the digestive system, occurring primarily in the large intestine (colon). This process involves the absorption of water and electrolytes, fermentation by gut bacteria, and the eventual elimination of waste products. The mechanism of defecation involves coordinated muscular contractions and neural control.

Formation of Faeces

1. Passage from the Small Intestine :

- After digestion in the small intestine, partially digested food (chyme) enters the large intestine. Here, further processing occurs as water and electrolytes are absorbed.

2. Water Absorption :

- The large intestine absorbs approximately 1 to 2 litres of water daily from the chyme, which is essential for maintaining fluid balance in the body. This absorption transforms the liquid chyme into a more solid form.

3. Fermentation by Gut Bacteria :

- The colon houses a diverse microbiota that plays a significant role in faeces formation. Bacteria ferment undigested carbohydrates (such as cellulose) and produce short-chain fatty acids, gases, and vitamins (e.g., vitamin K and biotin) as by-products.
- This fermentation process contributes to the bulk of faecal matter and influences its composition.

4. Composition of Faeces :

- Faeces consist of about 75% water and 25% solid material, which includes:
- Undigested food components (approximately 30% cellulose).
- Bacteria (about 30%).
- Inorganic substances (10-20%).
- Cholesterol and fats (10-20%).
- Protein (2-3%).

- The brown colour of faeces is primarily due to stercobilin, a product formed from bilirubin by bacterial action.

5. Storage :

- Once formed, faeces are stored in the rectum until defecation occurs. The rectum can accommodate a certain volume of faecal material before signalling the need for elimination.

Mechanism of Defecation

Defecation is the process by which faeces are expelled from the body. It involves several steps:

1. Filling of the Rectum :

- As faeces accumulate in the rectum, stretch receptors in its walls are activated, sending signals to the brain that create the urge to defecate.

2. Coordination of Muscles :

- The defecation reflex involves both involuntary and voluntary muscle contractions:
- Involuntary Control : The internal anal sphincter (smooth muscle) relaxes reflexively when rectal pressure increases.
- Voluntary Control : The external anal sphincter (skeletal muscle) can be consciously controlled to either facilitate or delay defecation.

3. Increased Intra-abdominal Pressure :

- To aid in expelling faeces, individuals may perform the Valsalva maneuver, which involves closing the mouth and pinching the nose while bearing down to increase intra-abdominal pressure.
- Contraction of abdominal muscles also contributes to this pressure increase.

4. Expulsion of Faeces :

- When ready to defecate, the external anal sphincter relaxes, allowing faeces to exit through the anus.
- The coordinated contraction of the rectal muscles propels faeces out of the body.

Chapter – 13

(13.1) Physiology of special senses Physiology of sleep and dreams

Physiology of Special Senses

The special senses are specific sensory systems that have dedicated organs for processing particular types of stimuli. These include vision, hearing, taste, smell, and equilibrium (balance). Each sense has unique physiological mechanisms and pathways for transmitting sensory information to the brain.

1. Vision

- Organ : Eyes

- Mechanism :
- Light enters the eye through the cornea, passes through the lens, and is focused on the retina.
- Photoreceptors (rods and cones) in the retina convert light into electrical signals.
- Signals are transmitted via the optic nerve to the visual cortex in the occipital lobe for processing.

The physiology of the eye involves how the eye captures light, converts it into electrical signals, and sends these signals to the brain for interpretation as vision. Here's a breakdown of the key structures and their functions:

Optic Nerve	Transmits electrical signals from the retina to the brain.
Macula	A central part of the retina responsible for sharp, detailed central vision.
Fovea	The central point in the macula with the highest concentration of cones, providing sharp vision.
Sclera	The white outer layer that protects the eye and provides attachment points for muscles.
Choroid	A vascular layer supplying oxygen and nutrients to the retina.
Iris	The colored part of the eye, a muscle that adjusts pupil size based on light intensity.
Lens	A flexible, transparent structure that fine-tunes focus by changing its shape (accommodation).
Vitreous Humor	A gel-like substance that fills the eyeball, maintaining shape and allowing light to pass through.
Retina	A layer at the back of the eye containing photoreceptor cells that detect light.
Optic Nerve	Transmits electrical signals from the retina to the brain.

The Process of Vision

1. Light Entry and Focusing :
   - Light enters the eye through the cornea , which bends (refracts) the light.
   - The lens adjusts its shape (accommodation) to focus light onto the retina.

2. Formation of the Image :
   - The light is focused onto the retina, forming an inverted image on the photoreceptors (rods and cones).

3. Phototransduction :
   - Photoreceptors in the retina convert light into electrical signals:
     - Rods : Sensitive to dim light, responsible for night vision and peripheral vision.
     - Cones : Sensitive to bright light and colour, concentrated in the fovea for sharp central vision.
   - Light activates the photopigments (rhodopsin in rods and opsins in cones) triggering a chemical cascade.

4. Signal Processing :
   - The electrical signals from photoreceptors are processed by bipolar cells and ganglion cells in the retina.
   - Signals are transmitted via the optic nerve.

5. Transmission to the Brain :
   - The optic nerve carries the signals to the optic chiasm, where information from the nasal halves of the retina crosses to the opposite side of the brain.
   - Signals are relayed to the visual cortex in the occipital lobe via the thalamus.

6. Image Interpretation :
   - The brain processes the electrical signals, integrates them with past experiences, and creates the perception of an upright, coloured, and detailed visual image.

Key Physiological Mechanisms

- Accommodation : The lens changes shape to focus on objects at varying distances.
- Pupillary Reflex : The pupil constricts in bright light (parasympathetic response) and dilates in dim light (sympathetic response).
- Photoreceptor Adaptation : The retina adapts to different light levels (dark and light adaptation).
- Binocular Vision : The brain integrates images from both eyes to provide depth perception and a three-dimensional view.

Common Disorders

- Myopia (Near-sightedness) : Light focuses in front of the retina, causing difficulty seeing distant objects.
- Hyperopia (Farsightedness) : Light focuses behind the retina, causing difficulty seeing close objects.
- Astigmatism : Irregular curvature of the cornea or lens distorts vision.
- Cataracts : Clouding of the lens impairs light passage.
- Glaucoma : Increased intraocular pressure damages the optic nerve.
- Macular Degeneration : Damage to the macula affects central vision.

This overview explains how the eye works as a highly specialized organ for vision, converting light into meaningful information for the brain.

2. Hearing

- Organ : Ears

- Mechanism :
- Sound waves enter through the external auditory canal and vibrate the tympanic membrane (eardrum).
- Vibrations are amplified by three tiny bones (ossicles) in the middle ear and transmitted to the cochlea in the inner ear.
- Hair cells in the cochlea convert mechanical vibrations into electrical signals sent via the auditory nerve to the auditory cortex in the temporal lobe.

Part of the Ear	Structure	Function
Outer Ear	Pinna (Auricle)	Captures and funnels sound waves into the ear canal.
	External Auditory Canal	Transmits sound waves to the eardrum and amplifies certain frequencies.
	Tympanic Membrane (Eardrum)	Vibrates in response to sound waves, converting them into mechanical energy.
Middle Ear	Ossicles (Malleus, Incus, Stapes)	Amplify and transmit vibrations from the eardrum to the oval window of the inner ear.
	Eustachian Tube	Equalizes pressure between the middle ear and the environment for proper vibration.
Inner Ear	Cochlea	Contains sensory cells (hair cells) that convert mechanical energy into electrical signals.
	Semicircular Canals	Not involved in hearing but assist with balance.
	Vestibulocochlear Nerve (Cranial Nerve VIII)	Transmits electrical signals from the cochlea to the brain.
Central Auditory Pathway	Auditory Cortex (Temporal Lobe)	Processes and interprets sound information.

The physiology of hearing involves the process of capturing sound waves, converting them into mechanical, then electrical signals, and transmitting these signals to the brain for interpretation. Here's an overview of the structures and their roles in hearing:

The Process of Hearing

1. Sound Wave Collection (Outer Ear):

- Sound waves are captured by the pinna and directed into the external auditory canal.

- The tympanic membrane vibrates in response to sound waves, converting air vibrations into mechanical vibrations.

2. Amplification and Transmission (Middle Ear):

- The ossicles (malleus, incus, stapes) amplify the vibrations and transfer them to the oval window, a membrane separating the middle ear from the inner ear.
- The stapes pushes against the oval window, generating waves in the fluid of the cochlea.

3. Conversion to Electrical Signals (Inner Ear):

- In the cochlea, vibrations create waves in the perilymph and endolymph (fluids within the cochlea).
- These waves stimulate the basilar membrane, causing it to vibrate at specific points depending on the frequency of the sound:
  - High-frequency sounds stimulate the base of the cochlea.
  - Low-frequency sounds stimulate the apex of the cochlea.
- The movement of the basilar membrane causes the hair cells in the organ of Corti to bend against the tectorial membrane.
- Bending of hair cells opens ion channels, causing the release of neurotransmitters and generating electrical signals.

4. Transmission to the Brain:

- The electrical signals are transmitted via the auditory nerve (part of the vestibulocochlear nerve) to the brainstem.
- From the brainstem, signals are relayed through the inferior colliculus and thalamus (medial geniculate nucleus) to the auditory cortex in the temporal lobe.

5.Sound Perception:

- The auditory cortex processes the signals to identify pitch, loudness, and location of the sound.
- The brain integrates this information with past experiences to interpret the sound.

Key Mechanisms

- Frequency Coding : The location of hair cell activation on the basilar membrane encodes pitch.
- Intensity Coding : The amplitude of basilar membrane movement determines loudness.
- Localization : The brain uses differences in time and intensity of sound arrival at both ears to localize the source.

Disorders of Hearing

1. Conductive Hearing Loss : Problems in the outer or middle ear (e.g., earwax blockage, otitis media, ossicle damage).
2. Sensorineural Hearing Loss : Damage to the cochlea or auditory nerve (e.g., noise exposure, aging).
3. Tinnitus : Perception of ringing or buzzing in the ears without external sound.
4. Presbycusis : Age-related hearing loss, typically affecting high frequencies.

The physiology of hearing showcases the intricate process of transforming sound waves into meaningful information that allows us to perceive and interact with our auditory environment.

3. Taste (Gustation)

- Organ : Tongue

- Mechanism :
- Taste buds on the tongue contain chemoreceptors that respond to dissolved substances.
- There are five primary taste modalities: sweet, sour, salty, bitter, and umami.
- Signals from taste buds travel via cranial nerves to the gustatory cortex for interpretation.

The physiology of taste involves detecting chemical compounds in food and beverages and interpreting them as distinct taste sensations. This process occurs through specialized sensory cells located on the tongue and other areas of the oral cavity.

Structure	Function
Taste Buds	Contain taste receptor cells responsible for detecting specific taste molecules.
Papillae	Structures on the tongue housing taste buds. Types:
	- **Fungiform Papillae:** Found on the front of the tongue, contain a few taste buds.
	- **Circumvallate Papillae:** Large, located at the back of the tongue, contain many taste buds.
	- **Foliate Papillae:** On the sides of the tongue, also contain taste buds.
	- **Filiform Papillae:** Do not contain taste buds; involved in texture perception.
Taste Receptor Cells	Detect specific taste molecules and generate signals.
Cranial Nerves	Transmit taste signals to the brain:
	- **Facial Nerve (CN VII):** Anterior two-thirds of the tongue.
	- **Glossopharyngeal Nerve (CN IX):** Posterior one-third of the tongue.
	- **Vagus Nerve (CN X):** ↓ te from the epiglottis and pharynx.
Brain Regions	Process taste signals:
	- **Nucleus of the Solitary Tract (Medulla):** Initial relay station.
	- **Thalamus:** Relays signals to the cerebral cortex.
	- **Primary Gustatory Cortex (Insula and Frontal Operculum):** Perception of taste.

The Process of Taste Perception

1. Taste Molecule Detection:

- Taste molecules from food dissolve in saliva.
- These molecules interact with taste receptor cells located in taste buds.

2. Activation of Taste Receptors:

- Taste receptor cells have specialized proteins on their membranes to detect specific tastes:
- Sweet : Activated by sugars (e.g., glucose, sucrose) through G-protein-coupled receptors (GPCRs).
- Salty : Triggered by sodium ions (Na^+) entering ion channels.
- Sour : Activated by hydrogen ions (H^+) from acids interacting with ion channels.
- Bitter : Detected by bitter compounds via GPCRs, often as a warning for toxins.
- Umami : Triggered by amino acids like glutamate (e.g., in MSG) through GPCRs.

3. Signal Transmission:

- Binding of taste molecules generates an electrical signal in the taste receptor cell.
- The signal is transmitted to the brain via cranial nerves:
  - Facial Nerve (CN VII) for the front of the tongue.
  - Glossopharyngeal Nerve (CN IX) for the back of the tongue.
  - Vagus Nerve (CN X) for taste from the throat.

4. Signal Processing in the Brain:

- Signals travel to the nucleus of the solitary tract in the brainstem.
- From there, they are relayed to the thalamus and then to the primary gustatory cortex in the insula and frontal operculum.

5. Perception of Taste:

- The brain integrates taste signals with other sensory inputs (smell, texture, temperature) to produce the overall flavour perception.

Types of Tastes

1. Sweet : Indicates energy-rich nutrients.
2. Salty : Detects electrolytes (e.g., sodium).
3. Sour : Alerts to acidity, potentially harmful substances.
4. Bitter : Often associated with toxic substances.
5. Umami : Detects savoury tastes, signalling protein-rich foods.

Factors Influencing Taste Perception

- Age : Taste sensitivity declines with age.
- Temperature : Warm foods enhance sweet and salty tastes.
- Smell : Closely linked to taste; loss of smell diminishes flavour perception.
- Health Conditions : Conditions like colds, medications, or damage to cranial nerves can impair taste.

Disorders of Taste

1. Ageusia : Complete loss of taste.
2. Hypogeusia : Reduced taste sensitivity.
3. Dysgeusia : Distorted taste perception (e.g., metallic or foul taste).

The physiology of taste illustrates how the body detects and interprets chemical stimuli, allowing us to enjoy food and identify substances that are nutritious or potentially harmful.

4. Smell (Olfaction)

- Organ : Nasal passages

- Mechanism :
  - Odour molecules bind to olfactory receptors in the nasal epithelium.
  - This binding generates electrical signals that are transmitted via the olfactory nerve to the olfactory bulb and then to higher brain regions for processing.

Structure	Function
Nasal Cavity	Warms, humidifies, and filters air; contains the olfactory epithelium.
Olfactory Epithelium	Specialized tissue in the upper nasal cavity that contains sensory receptor cells.
Olfactory Receptor Cells	Detect odor molecules; neurons with specialized receptors located in the olfactory epithelium.
Olfactory Bulb	First processing center for olfactory signals in the brain.
Olfactory Nerve (CN I)	Transmits electrical signals from the olfactory receptor cells to the olfactory bulb.
Olfactory Tract	Carries processed signals from the olfactory bulb to higher brain regions.
Limbic System	Processes emotional and memory-related aspects of smell (includes the amygdala and hippocampus).
Primary Olfactory Cortex	Located in the temporal lobe; interprets and identifies smells.

The physiology of smell, or olfaction, involves the detection of airborne chemical molecules, their conversion into electrical signals, and their interpretation by the brain as specific odours. Here's an overview:

The Process of Smell Perception

1. Odorant Molecule Detection:

- Airborne odour molecules (odorants) enter the nasal cavity during inhalation.
- Odorants dissolve in the mucus layer of the olfactory epithelium.

2. Activation of Olfactory Receptor Cells:

- The olfactory receptor neurons in the epithelium have cilia with odorant receptor proteins.
- Odorants bind to specific receptor proteins on the cilia, triggering a G-protein-coupled receptor (GPCR) mechanism.

- This mechanism generates an electrical signal (action potential) in the receptor cell.

3. Signal Transmission to the Brain:

- The action potential travels along the axons of the olfactory receptor cells, which form the olfactory nerve (cranial nerve I).
- The nerve transmits signals to the olfactory bulb.

4. Processing in the Olfactory Bulb:

- Within the olfactory bulb, signals are organized and processed in structures called glomeruli.
- Each glomerulus corresponds to a specific odorant receptor type.
- Mitral and tufted cells in the bulb refine and relay the signals to the brain via the olfactory tract.

5. Interpretation in the Brain:

- Signals are transmitted to the primary olfactory cortex in the temporal lobe for identification of the smell.
- Additional processing occurs in the orbitofrontal cortex, integrating smell with other sensory inputs like taste.
- Connections to the limbic system (e.g., amygdala and hippocampus) link smell to emotions and memories.

Unique Features of the Olfactory System

- Direct Brain Pathway : Unlike other sensory systems, olfactory signals bypass the thalamus and go directly to the brain.
- High Sensitivity : The human nose can detect thousands of different odorants, even in minute concentrations.
- Adaptation : Prolonged exposure to an odour reduces sensitivity to that odour (olfactory adaptation).

Factors Affecting Smell

- Age : Olfactory sensitivity declines with age.
- Health : Conditions like colds, allergies, or sinus infections can block the nasal cavity and reduce smell.
- Damage : Trauma to the olfactory nerve or brain regions can impair or eliminate smell.
- Environment : Exposure to strong odours can temporarily desensitize receptors.

Disorders of Smell

1. Anosmia : Complete loss of smell.
2. Hyposmia : Reduced ability to detect odours.
3. Parosmia : Distorted perception of smells (e.g., pleasant smells perceived as unpleasant).
4. Phantosmia : Smelling odours that are not present.

The physiology of smell enables humans to detect and interpret a vast range of chemical stimuli in the environment, contributing to flavour perception, environmental awareness, and emotional experiences.

5. Equilibrium (Balance)

- Organ : Inner ear

- Mechanism :
  - The vestibular system consists of semi-circular canals and otolith organs that detect changes in head position and movement.
  - Hair cells within these structures respond to fluid movement and gravitational forces, sending signals to the brain about balance and spatial orientation.

System	Structure	Function
Vestibular System	Semicircular Canals	Detect rotational (angular) movements of the head.
	Otolith Organs (Utricle, Saccule)	Detect linear accelerations and head position relative to gravity.
	Vestibular Nerve	Transmits signals from the inner ear to the brain.
Visual System	Eyes and Visual Pathways	Provide visual cues about the body's position in space.
Proprioceptive System	Muscle Spindles, Joint Receptors	Provide information about body and limb position.
Central Processing	Cerebellum	Coordinates balance and motor responses.
	Brainstem (Vestibular Nuclei)	Integrates signals from the vestibular, visual, and proprioceptive systems.

The Process of Maintaining Balance

1. Sensory Input:

- Rotational Movements (Semi-circular Canals):
  - Each of the three semi-circular canals detects rotational motion in a specific plane.
  - Endolymph fluid within the canals moves in response to head rotation, bending hair cells in the ampullae (sensory regions).
  - Bending of hair cells opens ion channels, generating nerve impulses.

- Linear Movements and Gravity (Otolith Organs):
  - The utricle and saccule detect linear acceleration and head tilt.
  - Tiny crystals (otoliths) rest on a gelatinous layer above hair cells. Movement displaces the otoliths, bending hair cells and generating signals.

- Visual Inputs :
  - Eyes track the environment to provide cues about orientation and motion.

- Proprioceptive Inputs :
  - Sensory receptors in muscles, tendons, and joints provide feedback about body position.

2. Signal Integration :
- Signals from the vestibular, visual, and proprioceptive systems are integrated in the vestibular nuclei of the brainstem and the cerebellum.
- The cerebellum processes this information to maintain balance and coordinate movements.

3. Motor Response :
- Adjustments are made to maintain equilibrium:
  - Vestibule-ocular Reflex (VOR) : Stabilizes vision by adjusting eye movements in response to head movements.
  - Postural Adjustments : Muscle contractions adjust body position to maintain stability.

Disorder	Description
Vertigo	Sensation of spinning or movement caused by vestibular dysfunction.
Motion Sickness	Mismatch between vestibular and visual inputs.
Benign Paroxysmal Positional Vertigo (BPPV)	Displacement of otoliths into semicircular canals, causing brief episodes of vertigo.
Meniere's Disease	Inner ear disorder causing vertigo, hearing loss, tinnitus, and a feeling of fullness in the ear.
Vestibular Neuritis	Inflammation of the vestibular nerve, leading to sudden vertigo and imbalance.

Summary of Key Mechanisms

1. Vestibular System : Detects rotational and linear movements.
2. Integration : Combines sensory inputs to determine the body's position and movement.
3. Output : Coordinates motor responses to maintain balance and posture.

This integrated system allows humans to maintain equilibrium during a variety of activities, including standing, walking, and dynamic movements.

Summary of Special Senses

Sense	Organ	Stimulus Type	Mechanism of Signal Transduction
Vision	Eyes	Light	Photoreceptors convert light into electrical signals
Hearing	Ears	Sound	Hair cells convert vibrations into electrical signals
Taste	Tongue	Chemicals (taste)	Chemoreceptors in taste buds generate signals
Smell	Nasal passages	Chemicals (odor)	Olfactory receptors convert odor molecules into signals
Equilibrium	Inner ear	Movement/Gravity	Hair cells detect fluid movement and position changes

Physiology of Sleep and Dreams

The physiology of sleep and dreams involves a complex interplay of brain regions, neurotransmitters, and biological rhythms that regulate sleep states and dreaming. Sleep is essential for physical restoration, cognitive function, and emotional regulation.

1. Phases of Sleep

Sleep consists of two main phases:

1. Non-Rapid Eye Movement (NREM) Sleep
   - Divided into three stages (N1, N2, N3), progressing from light to deep sleep.

2. Rapid Eye Movement (REM) Sleep
   - Associated with vivid dreaming and active brain activity.

Sleep Cycle

- A full sleep cycle lasts about 90-120 minutes, alternating between NREM and REM sleep.
- An individual experiences 4-6 cycles per night.

System	Structure	Function
Circadian Rhythm	Suprachiasmatic Nucleus (SCN)	Located in the hypothalamus; regulates the sleep-wake cycle based on light and darkness.
Neurotransmitters	GABA (Inhibitory)	Promotes sleep by reducing brain activity.
	Orexin (Hypocretin)	Promotes wakefulness; its dysfunction is linked to narcolepsy.
	Melatonin	Released by the pineal gland in response to darkness; promotes sleep onset.
Sleep-Promoting Centers	Ventrolateral Preoptic Area (VLPO)	Inhibits arousal systems during sleep.
Arousal Systems	Reticular Activating System (RAS)	Promotes wakefulness and alertness.

Stages of Sleep

1. NREM Sleep

- Stage N1 (Light Sleep) :
  - Transition between wakefulness and sleep.
  - Brain activity slows; muscles relax.
  - Theta waves dominate.

- **Stage N2 (Intermediate Sleep) :**
  - Body temperature drops; heart rate slows.
  - Sleep spindles (bursts of brain activity) and K-complexes (large brain waves) appear.
  - Represents 50% of total sleep.

- **Stage N3 (Deep Sleep) :**
  - Known as slow-wave sleep (SWS).
  - Delta waves dominate.
  - Essential for physical restoration, tissue repair, and immune function.

2. REM Sleep

- Occurs approximately 90 minutes after sleep onset.
- Brain Activity : High; similar to wakefulness (beta waves).

- Physical State :
  - Muscle atonia (paralysis of voluntary muscles) to prevent acting out dreams.
  - Rapid eye movements.

- Functions :
  - Memory consolidation.
  - Emotional processing.
  - Vivid dreaming.

Physiology of Dreams

- Dreams occur primarily during REM sleep, though they can also happen in NREM stages.
- Brain Regions Involved :
  - Limbic System : Emotional content of dreams (e.g., amygdala and hippocampus).
  - Prefrontal Cortex : Less active during REM, leading to reduced logic and self-awareness in dreams.
  - Visual Cortex : Generates imagery in dreams.
  - Neurotransmitters in REM Sleep :
  - Acetylcholine : High; promotes brain activity.
  - Norepinephrine and Serotonin : Low; contributes to the dream state.

Functions of Sleep and Dreams

Sleep Function	Description
Restoration and Recovery	Repairs tissues, supports immune function, and restores energy.
Memory Consolidation	Strengthens neural connections and integrates new memories.
Emotional Regulation	Processes emotional experiences and reduces stress.
Dream Function	- Problem-solving and creativity.
	- Emotional catharsis: processing unresolved emotions.

Sleep Disorders

Disorder	Description
Insomnia	Difficulty falling or staying asleep.
Sleep Apnea	Interrupted breathing during sleep due to airway obstruction or central nervous system issues.
Narcolepsy	Excessive daytime sleepiness and sudden REM sleep attacks.
Parasomnias	Unusual behaviors during sleep (e.g., sleepwalking, night terrors).
Restless Legs Syndrome	Uncomfortable sensations in the legs causing an urge to move them, disrupting sleep.

Dream Theories

1. Activation-Synthesis Hypothesis :
   - Dreams are the brain's attempt to make sense of random neural activity during REM sleep.
2. Information-Processing Theory :
   - Dreams help consolidate memories and solve problems.
3. Psychoanalytic Theory (Freud) :
   - Dreams reflect unconscious desires and emotions.

Sleep and dreams are crucial for overall health, playing a vital role in physical restoration, emotional balance, and cognitive function.

Multiple Choice Questions

Here are multiple-choice questions (MCQs) based on the given topics:

Chapter – 1 Physiology Homeostasis

1. **What is homeostasis?**
   A) The process of cell division
   B) Maintenance of a stable internal environment
   C) Breakdown of glucose for energy
   D) Production of proteins
2. **Which of the following systems plays a major role in maintaining homeostasis?**
   A) Nervous system
   B) Endocrine system
   C) Both A and B
   D) Skeletal system
3. **Which mechanism is involved in the maintenance of homeostasis?**
   A) Positive feedback loop
   B) Negative feedback loop
   C) Both A and B
   D) None of the above
4. **What is the basic structural and functional unit of life?**
   A) Organelle
   B) Cell
   C) Tissue
   D) Organ
5. **What is the function of the cell membrane?**
   A) Generate ATP
   B) Act as a barrier and regulate transport
   C) Replicate DNA
   D) None of the above
6. **Which molecule forms the bilayer structure of the cell membrane?**
   A) Proteins
   B) Lipids
   C) Carbohydrates
   D) Nucleotides

1- B,	2- C,	3- C,	4- B,	5- B,	6- B,

7. **What type of transport does not require energy?**
   A) Active transport
   B) Passive transport
   C) Endocytosis
   D) Exocytosis
8. **Which transport mechanism moves substances against their concentration gradient?**
   A) Diffusion
   B) Osmosis
   C) Active transport
   D) Facilitated diffusion
9. **What is osmosis?**
   A) Movement of solute particles
   B) Movement of water across a semi-permeable membrane
   C) Transport of proteins
   D) Active movement of ions
10. **Facilitated diffusion involves:**
   A) Energy expenditure
   B) Protein channels or carriers
   C) Simple movement across the lipid bilayer
   D) None of the above
11. **What maintains the resting membrane potential?**
   A) Sodium-potassium pump
   B) Calcium ions
   C) ATP synthesis
   D) Endocytosis
12. **What is the typical value of resting membrane potential in neurons?**
   A) +70 mV
   B) -70 mV
   C) 0 mV
   D) -20 mV
13. **What causes depolarization during an action potential?**
   A) Influx of Na^+ ions
   B) Efflux of K^+ ions
   C) Influx of Cl^- ions
   D) None of the above
14. **The repolarization phase of an action potential is due to:**
   A) Opening of Na^+ channels
   B) Opening of K^+ channels
   C) Closing of K^+ channels
   D) Opening of Cl^- channels

7- B,	8- C,	9- B,	10- B,	11- A,	12- B,	13- A,	14- B

15. **What is the normal pH of human blood?**
    A) 6.8
    B) 7.4
    C) 7.0
    D) 8.0
16. **Which buffer system is the most important in maintaining blood pH?**
    A) Phosphate buffer system
    B) Protein buffer system
    C) Bicarbonate buffer system
    D) Ammonia buffer system
17. **Which electrolyte is the major cation in extracellular fluid?**
    A) Potassium (K^+)
    B) Sodium (Na^+)
    C) Calcium (Ca^{2+})
    D) Magnesium (Mg^{2+})
18. **What hormone regulates water balance by affecting kidney function?**
    A) Insulin
    B) Aldosterone
    C) Antidiuretic hormone (ADH)
    D) Cortisol
19. **Hypernatremia refers to:**
    A) Low sodium levels in the blood
    B) High sodium levels in the blood
    C) Low potassium levels in the blood
    D) High potassium levels in the blood
20. **Which macronutrient is the primary source of energy?**
    A) Proteins
    B) Fats
    C) Carbohydrates
    D) Vitamins
21. **Which of the following is a complete protein?**
    A) Rice
    B) Wheat
    C) Soy
    D) Corn
22. **What is the primary function of dietary fiber?**
    A) Energy production
    B) Building muscle
    C) Improving digestive health
    D) Synthesizing enzymes

15- B,	16- C,	17- B,	18- C,	19- B,	20- C,	21- C,	22- C

Chapter – 2 Physiology of Respiratory system

1. **What is the primary function of the respiratory system?**
   A) Digestion of food
   B) Exchange of gases between the body and the environment
   C) Regulation of blood pressure
   D) Production of hormones
2. **Which of the following is part of the upper respiratory tract?**
   A) Lungs
   B) Trachea
   C) Nasal cavity
   D) Bronchi
3. **The alveoli are:**
   A) The primary site for gas exchange
   B) The passageway for air to the lungs
   C) Muscles involved in respiration
   D) Blood vessels in the lungs
4. **Ventilation refers to:**
   A) Gas exchange in the alveoli
   B) Movement of air in and out of the lungs
   C) Transport of oxygen in the blood
   D) Cellular respiration
5. **During inspiration, the diaphragm:**
   A) Contracts and moves downward
   B) Relaxes and moves upward
   C) Stays stationary
   D) Contracts and moves upward
6. **Which of the following is a passive process in normal respiration?**
   A) Inspiration
   B) Expiration
   C) Both inspiration and expiration
   D) None of the above
7. **Gas exchange occurs primarily in the:**
   A) Trachea
   B) Bronchi
   C) Bronchioles
   D) Alveoli
8. **Which gas has the highest partial pressure in the atmosphere?**
   A) Oxygen
   B) Carbon dioxide
   C) Nitrogen
   D) Argon

1- B,	2- C,	3- A,	4- B,	5- A,	6- B,	7- D,	8- C

9. **Hemoglobin transports oxygen by binding to:**
   A) Iron in the heme group
   B) Globin protein
   C) Carbon dioxide molecules
   D) Nitrogen molecules
10. **Most carbon dioxide in the blood is transported as:**
   A) Dissolved CO_2
   B) Bicarbonate ions
   C) Carbaminohemoglobin
   D) Free carbon dioxide gas
11. **The respiratory center is located in the:**
   A) Cerebellum
   B) Medulla oblongata and pons
   C) Hypothalamus
   D) Cerebrum
12. **Which chemical primarily stimulates an increase in respiration?**
   A) Low oxygen levels
   B) High carbon dioxide levels
   C) Low nitrogen levels
   D) High water vapor levels
13. **Artificial respiration is used to:**
   A) Stop breathing in emergencies
   B) Assist or restore normal breathing
   C) Reduce the rate of respiration
   D) Decrease oxygen supply to tissues
14. **Asphyxia refers to:**
   A) Increased oxygen levels in the blood
   B) Insufficient oxygen supply due to obstruction of airways
   C) Excessive oxygen in tissues
   D) Reduced carbon dioxide levels in the blood
15. **Which type of hypoxia is caused by inadequate oxygen supply to tissues despite normal oxygen levels in the blood?**
   A) Hypoxemic hypoxia
   B) Anaemic hypoxia
   C) Stagnant hypoxia
   D) Histotoxic hypoxia

9- A,	10- B,	11- B,	12- B,	13- B,	14- B,	15- D

Chapter - 3 Physiology of Gastrointestinal system

1. **The gastrointestinal tract starts and ends at the:**
   A) Mouth and rectum
   B) Mouth and anus
   C) Pharynx and rectum
   D) Oesophagus and anus
2. **Which part of the GI tract is primarily responsible for nutrient absorption?**
   A) Stomach
   B) Small intestine
   C) Large intestine
   D) Oesophagus
3. **The primary function of the large intestine is:**
   A) Protein digestion
   B) Absorption of water and electrolytes
   C) Absorption of fats
   D) Breakdown of carbohydrates
4. **Which enzyme in saliva begins carbohydrate digestion?**
   A) Lipase
   B) Pepsin
   C) Amylase
   D) Protease
5. **The primary component of gastric juice responsible for protein digestion is:**
   A) Hydrochloric acid (HCl)
   B) Pepsinogen/Pepsin
   C) Bicarbonate
   D) Mucus
6. **The pancreas secretes which enzyme for fat digestion?**
   A) Amylase
   B) Lipase
   C) Trypsin
   D) Pepsin
7. **Bile is essential for the digestion and absorption of:**
   A) Proteins
   B) Fats
   C) Carbohydrates
   D) Vitamins
8. **Which is a major function of the liver in digestion?**
   A) Production of bile
   B) Secretion of digestive enzymes
   C) Absorption of nutrients
   D) Neutralizing stomach acid

1- B,	2- B,	3- B,	4- C,	5- B,	6- B,	7- B,	8- A

9. **The stomach secretes intrinsic factor, which is essential for the absorption of:**
   A) Vitamin C
   B) Vitamin B12
   C) Vitamin D
   D) Iron
10. **The large intestine is involved in:**
   A) Production of bile
   B) Synthesis of digestive enzymes
   C) Absorption of vitamins like vitamin K
   D) Protein metabolism
11. **Deglutition refers to:**
   A) The movement of food from the stomach to the small intestine
   B) The act of swallowing
   C) The process of defecation
   D) Movement of food through the esophagus
12. **Peristalsis is controlled by:**
   A) Voluntary muscles
   B) The enteric nervous system
   C) The somatic nervous system
   D) None of the above
13. **Defecation is initiated by the:**
   A) Swallowing reflex
   B) Enteric nervous system
   C) Rectoanal reflex
   D) Gastric emptying reflex
14. **Protein digestion begins in the:**
   A) Mouth
   B) Stomach
   C) Small intestine
   D) Large intestine
15. **Carbohydrate metabolism in the body primarily provides:**
   A) Energy
   B) Structural proteins
   C) Hormonal precursors
   D) Lipid molecules

9- B,	10- C,	11- B,	12- B,	13- C,	14- B,	15- A

Chapter – 4 Physiology of Nervous System

1. **The nervous system is divided into:**
   A) Central and peripheral nervous systems
   B) Sympathetic and parasympathetic systems
   C) Voluntary and involuntary systems
   D) Sensory and motor systems
2. **Which is the functional unit of the nervous system?**
   A) Neuron
   B) Glial cell
   C) Dendrite
   D) Synapse
3. **The myelin sheath around axons is responsible for:**
   A) Generating electrical impulses
   B) Slowing down impulse conduction
   C) Increasing the speed of impulse conduction
   D) Stimulating neurotransmitter release
4. **Which ion is primarily involved in the depolarization phase of a nerve impulse?**
   A) Sodium (Na^+)
   B) Potassium (K^+)
   C) Calcium (Ca^{2+})
   D) Chloride (Cl^-)
5. **The synaptic cleft is:**
   A) The space between two neurons
   B) A component of the axon
   C) The site of electrical conduction
   D) The myelin sheath
6. **Which part of the CNS is responsible for maintaining posture and balance?**
   A) Cerebellum
   B) Medulla oblongata
   C) Thalamus
   D) Hypothalamus
7. **The peripheral nervous system consists of:**
   A) Brain and spinal cord
   B) Cranial and spinal nerves
   C) Sympathetic and parasympathetic systems
   D) None of the above
8. **The autonomic nervous system (ANS) controls:**
   A) Voluntary movements
   B) Skeletal muscle contraction
   C) Involuntary functions like heart rate and digestion
   D) Higher cognitive functions

1- A,	2- A,	3- C,	4- A,	5- A,	6- A,	7- B,	8- C

9. **Sensory nerves carry impulses:**
   A) To the brain and spinal cord
   B) Away from the brain and spinal cord
   C) To muscles and glands
   D) Between motor neurons
10. **Motor nerves control:**
    A) Reflex actions only
    B) Sensory processing
    C) Muscle contraction and glandular activity
    D) Special senses like vision
11. **The hypothalamus regulates:**
    A) Memory and learning
    B) Temperature, hunger, and thirst
    C) Voluntary motor control
    D) Visual and auditory processing
12. **Which part of the brain is primarily responsible for speech production?**
    A) Wernicke's area
    B) Broca's area
    C) Cerebellum
    D) Hippocampus
13. **Which brain structure is essential for memory formation?**
    A) Thalamus
    B) Cerebellum
    C) Hippocampus
    D) Medulla
14. **Rapid eye movement (REM) sleep is associated with:**
    A) Deep sleep and no dreams
    B) Light sleep and slow-wave brain activity
    C) Vivid dreaming and increased brain activity
    D) Reduced heart rate and no muscle activity
15. **EEG measures:**
    A) Blood flow in the brain
    B) Electrical activity of the brain
    C) Neurotransmitter levels
    D) Brainstem reflexes

9- A,	10- C,	11- B,	12- B,	13- C,	14- C,	15- B

Chapter - 5 Physiology of Endocrine glands

1. **The endocrine system primarily regulates:**
   A) Voluntary muscle contractions
   B) Homeostasis and long-term physiological processes
   C) Reflex actions
   D) The nervous system
2. **Endocrine glands release their secretions directly into:**
   A) The bloodstream
   B) Ducts
   C) Lymphatic vessels
   D) Body cavities

3. **Hormones can be classified into which major groups based on their structure?**
   A) Steroids, peptides, and amino acid derivatives
   B) Proteins, lipids, and carbohydrates
   C) Vitamins, enzymes, and lipids
   D) Sugars, acids, and bases
4. **Which of the following is a characteristic of hormones?**
   A) They act on specific target cells with matching receptors
   B) They are stored in large amounts in the bloodstream
   C) They work independently without feedback mechanisms
   D) They function only in the nervous system

5. **The anterior pituitary secretes:**
   A) Oxytocin and antidiuretic hormone (ADH)
   B) Growth hormone (GH) and thyroid-stimulating hormone (TSH)
   C) Insulin and glucagon
   D) Melatonin and calcitonin
6. **The hormone responsible for water reabsorption in the kidneys is:**
   A) Oxytocin
   B) Antidiuretic hormone (ADH)
   C) Cortisol
   D) Aldosterone

7. **The primary hormones produced by the thyroid gland are:**
   A) T3 (triiodothyronine) and T4 (thyroxine)
   B) Calcitonin and parathyroid hormone
   C) Insulin and glucagon
   D) Growth hormone and prolactin
8. **A deficiency of thyroid hormones in adults leads to:**
   A) Gigantism
   B) Myxedema
   C) Addison's disease
   D) Acromegaly

1- B,	2- A,	3- A,	4- A,	5- B,	6- B,	7- A,	8- B

9. **Parathyroid hormone (PTH) regulates:**
   A) Blood glucose levels
   B) Calcium and phosphate balance
   C) Water and electrolyte balance
   D) Blood pressure

10. **The pancreas is a mixed gland because it functions as:**
   A) An exocrine gland only
   B) An endocrine gland only
   C) Both endocrine and exocrine gland
   D) A paracrine gland
11. **Insulin primarily:**
   A) Increases blood glucose levels
   B) Decreases blood glucose levels
   C) Stimulates glycogen breakdown
   D) Inhibits fat storage

12. **The adrenal medulla secretes:**
   A) Glucocorticoids and mineralocorticoids
   B) Epinephrine and norepinephrine
   C) Insulin and glucagon
   D) Estrogen and progesterone
13. **Cortisol is a hormone produced by the adrenal cortex that:**
   A) Regulates sodium levels
   B) Promotes the stress response by increasing blood glucose
   C) Decreases heart rate
   D) Stimulates milk production

14. **Which gland secretes melatonin, regulating sleep-wake cycles?**
   A) Thyroid gland
   B) Pineal gland
   C) Adrenal gland
   D) Thymus gland
15. **The hormone responsible for the development of secondary sexual characteristics in males is:**
   A) Estrogen
   B) Progesterone
   C) Testosterone
   D) Prolactin

9- B,	10- C,	11- B,	12- B,	13- B,	14- B,	15- C

Chapter – 6 Haemopoetic system

1. **What is the primary function of red blood cells (RBCs)?**
   A) Fight infections
   B) Transport oxygen and carbon dioxide
   C) Aid in blood clotting
   D) Produce antibodies
2. **Which blood cells are primarily involved in immunity?**
   A) Platelets
   B) White blood cells (WBCs)
   C) Red blood cells (RBCs)
   D) Plasma cells
3. **What is the average lifespan of a red blood cell?**
   A) 60 days
   B) 90 days
   C) 120 days
   D) 150 days

4. **Haemopoiesis refers to:**
   A) The breakdown of hemoglobin
   B) The production of blood cells
   C) The clotting of blood
   D) The destruction of red blood cells
5. **Which organ is primarily responsible for haemopoiesis during fetal development?**
   A) Bone marrow
   B) Liver
   C) Spleen
   D) Thymus
6. **What is the stem cell responsible for all blood cell types?**
   A) Hemoglobin
   B) Hemocytoblast
   C) Myeloblast
   D) Lymphoblast

7. **The primary function of bone marrow is:**
   A) Storing minerals
   B) Producing blood cells
   C) Filtering blood
   D) Transporting nutrients
8. **Which type of bone marrow is active in blood cell production?**
   A) Red bone marrow
   B) Yellow bone marrow
   C) Both red and yellow bone marrow
   D) Compact bone

1- B,	2- B,	3- C,	4- B,	5- B,	6- B,	7- B,	8- A

9. **Haemoglobin is a protein responsible for:**
   A) Immunity
   B) Oxygen transport
   C) Blood clotting
   D) Hormone transport
10. **The iron-containing component of hemoglobin is called:**
   A) Globin
   B) Heme
   C) Ferritin
   D) Hemosiderin

11. **The first step in the blood clotting process is:**
   A) Platelet aggregation
   B) Vasoconstriction
   C) Fibrin formation
   D) Clot retraction
12. **Which vitamin is essential for blood clotting?**
   A) Vitamin A
   B) Vitamin C
   C) Vitamin D
   D) Vitamin K
13. **Heparin is an example of:**
   A) A clotting factor
   B) An anticoagulant
   C) A plasma protein
   D) A hormone

14. **The ABO blood group system is based on:**
   A) Antigens present on red blood cells
   B) Antibodies present in plasma
   C) Both antigens and antibodies
   D) Clotting factors in blood
15. **A person with blood group O is considered a universal donor because:**
   A) Their plasma contains no antibodies
   B) Their RBCs lack A and B antigens
   C) Their blood contains all antigens
   D) Their blood is compatible with all types

9- B,	10- B,	11- B,	12- D,	13- B,	14- C,	15- B

Chapter – 7 Immunity

1. **Which of the following is an example of innate immunity?**
   A) Vaccination
   B) Skin and mucous membranes
   C) Antibody production
   D) T-cell response
2. **Acquired immunity is characterized by:**
   A) Non-specific defense mechanisms
   B) The ability to recognize and respond to specific pathogens
   C) Immediate defense after birth
   D) The presence of natural barriers like skin
3. **Artificial immunity is achieved through:**
   A) Natural exposure to pathogens
   B) Genetic inheritance
   C) Vaccination or immunization
   D) Antibody production by the body

4. **Humoral immunity is primarily mediated by:**
   A) T-cells
   B) B-cells
   C) Phagocytes
   D) Natural killer cells
5. **The primary function of antibodies in humoral immunity is to:**
   A) Destroy infected cells
   B) Neutralize pathogens
   C) Activate T-cells
   D) Inhibit antigen presentation
6. **Which of the following is NOT a type of antibody (immunoglobulin)?**
   A) IgA
   B) IgG
   C) IgM
   D) IgT

7. **T-cell mediated immunity is primarily involved in:**
   A) Antibody production
   B) Destroying infected or abnormal cells
   C) Secretion of interferons
   D) Phagocytosis of pathogens
8. **Which of the following cells are involved in T-cell mediated immunity?**
   A) Helper T-cells (Th)
   B) Cytotoxic T-cells (Tc)
   C) Regulatory T-cells (Treg)
   D) All of the above

1- B,	2- B,	3- C,	4- B,	5- B,	6- D,	7- B,	8- D

9. **The major histocompatibility complex (MHC) molecules are involved in:**
   A) Presenting foreign antigens to T-cells
   B) Producing antibodies
   C) Producing cytokines
   D) Engulfing pathogens

10. **Hypersensitivity reactions are characterized by:**
   A) An overreaction of the immune system to harmless substances
   B) The body's failure to respond to pathogens
   C) Reduced immune response to infections
   D) A lack of antigen recognition by B-cells
11. **Type I hypersensitivity is also known as:**
   A) Cytotoxic hypersensitivity
   B) Immediate hypersensitivity
   C) Delayed-type hypersensitivity
   D) Immune complex-mediated hypersensitivity
12. **Anaphylaxis is a severe example of which type of hypersensitivity reaction?**
   A) Type I (Immediate) hypersensitivity
   B) Type II (Cytotoxic) hypersensitivity
   C) Type III (Immune complex-mediated) hypersensitivity
   D) Type IV (Delayed-type) hypersensitivity
13. **Type II hypersensitivity involves:**
   A) Antibodies binding to and destroying cells
   B) The formation of immune complexes in tissues
   C) A delayed T-cell response
   D) Mast cell degranulation
14. **Type IV hypersensitivity is mediated by:**
   A) IgE antibodies
   B) IgG antibodies
   C) T-cells
   D) Antigen-antibody complexes
15. **An example of a Type III hypersensitivity reaction is:**
   A) Asthma
   B) Rheumatoid arthritis
   C) Poison ivy rash
   D) Anaphylactic shock

9- A,	10- A,	11- B,	12- A,	13- A,	14- C,	15- B

Chapter – 8 Physiology of cardio-vascular system

1. **The primary function of the cardiovascular system is to:**
   A) Facilitate digestion
   B) Transport oxygen, nutrients, and waste products
   C) Produce hormones
   D) Control body temperature
2. **Which chamber of the heart receives oxygenated blood from the lungs?**
   A) Right atrium
   B) Left atrium
   C) Right ventricle
   D) Left ventricle
3. **The heart valves prevent:**
   A) Backflow of blood
   B) Mixing of oxygenated and deoxygenated blood
   C) Overfilling of the heart chambers
   D) Changes in heart rhythm
4. **The cardiac cycle consists of:**
   A) Two phases: systole and diastole
   B) One continuous contraction phase
   C) Four phases: atrial systole, atrial diastole, ventricular systole, ventricular diastole
   D) None of the above
5. **Ventricular systole refers to:**
   A) The relaxation of the ventricles
   B) The contraction of the ventricles
   C) The filling of the ventricles with blood
   D) The opening of the semilunar valves
6. **During diastole, the heart:**
   A) Pumps blood out of the ventricles
   B) Relaxes and fills with blood
   C) Generates electrical impulses
   D) Opens the semilunar valves
7. **The first heart sound (S1) is caused by:**
   A) Closure of the atrioventricular (AV) valves
   B) Closure of the semilunar valves
   C) Opening of the AV valves
   D) Blood entering the ventricles
8. **The second heart sound (S2) is associated with:**
   A) Closure of the AV valves
   B) Closure of the semilunar valves
   C) Opening of the semilunar valves
   D) Ventricular contraction

1- B,	2- B,	3- A,	4- A,	5- B,	6- B,	7- A,	8- B

9. **Cardiac output is defined as:**
   A) The amount of blood pumped by each ventricle in one minute
   B) The heart rate multiplied by venous return
   C) The total blood volume in the body
   D) The pressure exerted by the heart during systole
10. **The Frank-Starling law of the heart states that:**
   A) Cardiac output is independent of venous return
   B) Increased venous return increases the force of contraction
   C) Heart rate is controlled by oxygen demand
   D) The heart beats independently of external stimuli

11. **The P wave in an ECG represents:**
   A) Atrial depolarization
   B) Ventricular depolarization
   C) Atrial repolarization
   D) Ventricular repolarization
12. **The QRS complex in an ECG represents:**
   A) Atrial depolarization
   B) Ventricular depolarization
   C) Ventricular repolarization
   D) Atrial repolarization
13. **The T wave in an ECG corresponds to:**
   A) Ventricular repolarization
   B) Ventricular depolarization
   C) Atrial depolarization
   D) Atrial repolarization

14. **Heart rate is primarily regulated by:**
   A) The endocrine system
   B) The autonomic nervous system
   C) Blood glucose levels
   D) The Frank-Starling mechanism
15. **Which of the following hormones increases heart rate?**
   A) Insulin
   B) Adrenaline (epinephrine)
   C) Cortisol
   D) Thyroxine

9- A,	10- B,	11- A,	12- B,	13- A,	14- B,	15- B

Chapter – 9 Muscle Physiology

1. **Which type of muscle is under voluntary control?**
   A) Skeletal muscle
   B) Cardiac muscle
   C) Smooth muscle
   D) None of the above
2. **Cardiac muscles are characterized by:**
   A) Non-striated appearance
   B) Intercalated discs and striations
   C) Lack of a nucleus
   D) Voluntary control
3. **Smooth muscle is found in:**
   A) The heart
   B) Skeletal structures
   C) The walls of hollow organs
   D) The diaphragm
4. **Which type of muscle has the fastest contraction speed?**
   A) Smooth muscle
   B) Skeletal muscle
   C) Cardiac muscle
   D) All contract at the same speed
5. **The primary energy source for all muscle types is:**
   A) Lipids
   B) ATP
   C) Proteins
   D) Glucose

6. **The basic functional unit of a skeletal muscle is called a:**
   A) Myofibril
   B) Sarcomere
   C) Fascicle
   D) Tendon
7. **The role of calcium ions in muscle contraction is to:**
   A) Generate ATP
   B) Expose binding sites on actin filaments
   C) Break down acetylcholine
   D) Prevent actin-myosin interaction
8. **Which protein blocks the binding sites on actin filaments at rest?**
   A) Myosin
   B) Tropomyosin
   C) Troponin
   D) Titin

1- A,	2- B,	3- C,	4- B,	5- B,	6- B,	7- B,	8- B

9. **The neurotransmitter responsible for stimulating skeletal muscle contraction is:**
   A) Dopamine
   B) Acetylcholine
   C) Serotonin
   D) Norepinephrine
10. **In the sliding filament theory, muscle contraction occurs due to:**
   A) Actin and myosin filaments sliding past each other
   B) Shortening of actin filaments
   C) Shortening of myosin filaments
   D) Increase in sarcomere length

11. **Which type of muscle contraction is sustained and can last for long durations?**
   A) Skeletal muscle contraction
   B) Cardiac muscle contraction
   C) Smooth muscle contraction
   D) All muscle types
12. **Cardiac muscle contraction is regulated by:**
   A) The autonomic nervous system and intrinsic pacemaker cells
   B) The somatic nervous system
   C) Direct motor neuron stimulation
   D) Hormones only
13. **Which ion primarily triggers contraction in all muscle types?**
   A) Sodium
   B) Potassium
   C) Calcium
   D) Magnesium

14. **Which muscle type has gap junctions to facilitate coordinated contraction?**
   A) Skeletal muscle
   B) Cardiac muscle
   C) Smooth muscle
   D) Both cardiac and smooth muscle
15. **Which type of muscle exhibits the property of autorhythmicity?**
   A) Skeletal muscle
   B) Cardiac muscle
   C) Smooth muscle in the intestines
   D) Both B and C

9- B,	10- A,	11- C,	12- A,	13- C,	14- D,	15- D

Chapter – 10 Adipose Tissue

1. **The primary function of adipose tissue is to:**
   A) Store glycogen
   B) Store energy in the form of triglycerides
   C) Synthesize cholesterol
   D) Produce hormones
2. **Which lipoprotein is responsible for transporting triglycerides from the liver to peripheral tissues?**
   A) HDL
   B) LDL
   C) VLDL
   D) Chylomicrons
3. **Low-Density Lipoproteins (LDL) are often referred to as:**
   A) Good cholesterol
   B) Bad cholesterol
   C) Neutral cholesterol
   D) Essential cholesterol
4. **High-Density Lipoproteins (HDL) function to:**
   A) Transport triglycerides to adipose tissue
   B) Remove excess cholesterol from tissues and transport it to the liver
   C) Deliver cholesterol to cells for membrane synthesis
   D) Facilitate fat digestion
5. **The core of a lipoprotein particle is composed primarily of:**
   A) Proteins and cholesterol
   B) Triglycerides and cholesterol esters
   C) Phospholipids and free fatty acids
   D) Water and electrolytes
6. **Chylomicrons are primarily involved in the transport of:**
   A) Dietary cholesterol
   B) Dietary triglycerides
   C) Endogenous lipids
   D) Proteins

7. **The primary role of the skin in thermoregulation is:**
   A) Fat storage
   B) Sweating and vasodilation/vasoconstriction
   C) Sensory reception
   D) Vitamin D synthesis
8. **The outermost layer of the skin, responsible for protection, is called the:**
   A) Dermis
   B) Epidermis
   C) Hypodermis
   D) Subcutaneous layer

1- B,	2- C,	3- B,	4- B,	5- B,	6- B,	7- B,	8- B

9. **Which vitamin is synthesized in the skin upon exposure to sunlight?**
   A) Vitamin A
   B) Vitamin C
   C) Vitamin D
   D) Vitamin E
10. **The waterproofing property of the skin is due to the presence of:**
   A) Keratin
   B) Melanin
   C) Collagen
   D) Sebum

11. **The primary function of sweat glands is to:**
   A) Excrete waste products
   B) Regulate body temperature through evaporative cooling
   C) Lubricate the skin
   D) Produce vitamin D
12. **Which type of sweat gland is primarily responsible for thermoregulation?**
   A) Apocrine glands
   B) Sebaceous glands
   C) Eccrine glands
   D) Ceruminous glands
13. **Apocrine sweat glands are mainly found in:**
   A) Palms and soles
   B) Armpits and groin
   C) Forehead and scalp
   D) Chest and abdomen

14. **Sebaceous glands secrete:**
   A) Sweat
   B) Sebum
   C) Keratin
   D) Melanin
15. **The function of sebum is to:**
   A) Regulate body temperature
   B) Prevent microbial growth and keep the skin moisturized
   C) Facilitate sweat evaporation
   D) Synthesize keratin

9- C,	10- A,	11- B,	12- C,	13- B,	14- B,	15- B

Chapter – 11 Physiology of male and female reproductive

1. **Spermatogenesis occurs in the:**
   A) Epididymis
   B) Vas deferens
   C) Seminiferous tubules
   D) Prostate gland
2. **The process of spermatogenesis begins with:**
   A) Spermatids
   B) Primary spermatocytes
   C) Spermatogonia
   D) Secondary spermatocytes
3. **The hormone primarily responsible for stimulating spermatogenesis is:**
   A) Estrogen
   B) Progesterone
   C) Testosterone
   D) Prolactin
4. **How many functional sperm cells are produced from one primary spermatocyte?**
   A) 1
   B) 2
   C) 3
   D) 4

5. **Oogenesis occurs in the:**
   A) Oviduct
   B) Ovary
   C) Uterus
   D) Endometrium
6. **The primary oocyte remains arrested in which phase of meiosis until puberty?**
   A) Metaphase I
   B) Prophase I
   C) Anaphase II
   D) Telophase II
7. **How many mature ovum are produced from one primary oocyte?**
   A) 1
   B) 2
   C) 3
   D) 4

8. **Ovulation typically occurs on which day of a 28-day menstrual cycle?**
   A) Day 5
   B) Day 10
   C) Day 14
   D) Day 28

1- C,	2- C,	3- C,	4- D,	5- B,	6- B,	7- A,	8- C

9. **The hormone that triggers ovulation is:**
   A) Follicle-stimulating hormone (FSH)
   B) Luteinizing hormone (LH)
   C) Progesterone
   D) Estrogen
10. **During ovulation, the ruptured follicle transforms into:**
    A) A zygote
    B) A primary follicle
    C) A corpus luteum
    D) An antrum

11. **The menstrual cycle is regulated by hormones produced by the:**
    A) Adrenal gland
    B) Pituitary gland and ovaries
    C) Hypothalamus only
    D) Pancreas
12. **The proliferative phase of the menstrual cycle is dominated by:**
    A) Estrogen
    B) Progesterone
    C) Luteinizing hormone (LH)
    D) Follicle-stimulating hormone (FSH)
13. **The hormone responsible for maintaining the uterine lining during the luteal phase is:**
    A) Estrogen
    B) Progesterone
    C) FSH
    D) LH
14. **The shedding of the uterine lining occurs in the:**
    A) Follicular phase
    B) Ovulation phase
    C) Menstrual phase
    D) Luteal phase
15. **The absence of fertilization leads to a drop in which hormones, triggering menstruation?**
    A) Estrogen and progesterone
    B) FSH and LH
    C) Oxytocin and prolactin
    D) Testosterone and progesterone

9- B,	10- C,	11- B,	12- A,	13- B,	14- C,	15- A

Chapter – 12 Physiology of Excretion

1. **The functional unit of the kidney is called:**
   A) Glomerulus
   B) Bowman's capsule
   C) Nephron
   D) Renal pyramid
2. **Which structure transports urine from the kidney to the bladder?**
   A) Urethra
   B) Ureter
   C) Collecting duct
   D) Renal pelvis
3. **The urinary bladder stores urine and is lined by:**
   A) Simple squamous epithelium
   B) Transitional epithelium
   C) Cuboidal epithelium
   D) Stratified columnar epithelium

4. **The primary function of the kidney is to:**
   A) Regulate blood pressure
   B) Filter blood and form urine
   C) Store urine
   D) Produce bile
5. **The hormone secreted by the kidneys to stimulate red blood cell production is:**
   A) Renin
   B) Erythropoietin
   C) Aldosterone
   D) Antidiuretic hormone
6. **Which structure in the nephron is responsible for filtering blood plasma?**
   A) Proximal convoluted tubule
   B) Loop of Henle
   C) Glomerulus
   D) Collecting duct

7. **The process of urine formation involves all of the following EXCEPT:**
   A) Filtration
   B) Reabsorption
   C) Secretion
   D) Combustion
8. **Which part of the nephron is responsible for the reabsorption of glucose and amino acids?**
   A) Glomerulus
   B) Proximal convoluted tubule
   C) Distal convoluted tubule
   D) Loop of Henle

1- C,	2- B,	3- B,	4- B,	5- B,	6- C,	7- D,	8- B

9. **The countercurrent mechanism in the Loop of Henle is essential for:**
   A) Regulating blood pressure
   B) Concentrating urine
   C) Increasing glomerular filtration rate
   D) Stimulating aldosterone secretion
10. **The hormone responsible for water reabsorption in the kidneys is:**
    A) Aldosterone
    B) Antidiuretic hormone (ADH)
    C) Renin
    D) Cortisol

11. **The process of micturition is controlled by:**
    A) Voluntary and involuntary muscles
    B) Only voluntary muscles
    C) Only involuntary muscles
    D) Skeletal muscles
12. **The micturition reflex is coordinated by:**
    A) The brainstem and spinal cord
    B) The cerebellum
    C) The hypothalamus
    D) The pituitary gland

13. **The majority of water absorption in the large intestine occurs in the:**
    A) Cecum
    B) Colon
    C) Rectum
    D) Small intestine
14. **Which type of muscle is responsible for the movement of faeces through the colon?**
    A) Skeletal muscle
    B) Cardiac muscle
    C) Smooth muscle
    D) Striated muscle

15. **Defecation is initiated by the:**
    A) Micturition reflex
    B) Defecation reflex
    C) Countercurrent mechanism
    D) Peristaltic waves in the stomach

9- B,	10- B,	11- A,	12- A,	13- B,	14- C,	15- B

Chapter – 13 Special Senses, Sleep and Dreams

1. **The photoreceptor cells responsible for colour vision are:**
   A) Rods
   B) Cones
   C) Bipolar cells
   D) Ganglion cells
2. **The light-sensitive pigment in rods is called:**
   A) Rhodopsin
   B) Opsin
   C) Melanin
   D) Photopsin
3. **Accommodation in the eye refers to the ability to:**
   A) Adjust to different light intensities
   B) Focus on near and far objects
   C) Distinguish between colours
   D) Protect the retina

4. **The organ of Corti is located in the:**
   A) Cochlea
   B) Semicircular canals
   C) Tympanic membrane
   D) Vestibule
5. **The primary function of the Eustachian tube is to:**
   A) Amplify sound waves
   B) Maintain balance
   C) Equalize air pressure between the middle ear and the atmosphere
   D) Detect vibrations
6. **The auditory nerve carries signals to which part of the brain?**
   A) Cerebellum
   B) Occipital lobe
   C) Temporal lobe
   D) Frontal lobe

7. **Taste buds are primarily located on the:**
   A) Hard palate
   B) Tongue
   C) Soft palate
   D) Nasal cavity
8. **The sensation of taste is transmitted to the brain by all the following cranial nerves EXCEPT:**
   A) Facial nerve (CN VII)
   B) Glossopharyngeal nerve (CN IX)
   C) Vagus nerve (CN X)
   D) Hypoglossal nerve (CN XII)

1- B,	2- A,	3- B,	4- A,	5- C,	6- C,	7- B,	8- D

9. **Olfactory receptors are located in the:**
   A) Nasal septum
   B) Olfactory bulb
   C) Olfactory epithelium
   D) Nasopharynx
10. **The type of receptor responsible for detecting odors is:**
   A) Mechanoreceptor
   B) Chemoreceptor
   C) Photoreceptor
   D) Thermoreceptor

11. **Which part of the brain regulates sleep-wake cycles?**
   A) Cerebellum
   B) Hypothalamus
   C) Medulla oblongata
   D) Temporal lobe
12. **The hormone primarily involved in the regulation of sleep is:**
   A) Cortisol
   B) Melatonin
   C) Dopamine
   D) Adrenaline
13. **REM (Rapid Eye Movement) sleep is characterized by:**
   A) Deep, slow brain waves
   B) Dreaming and muscle paralysis
   C) No brain activity
   D) Increased heart rate and absence of dreams
14. **Non-REM sleep is divided into how many stages?**
   A) 2
   B) 3
   C) 4
   D) 5
15. **Sleepwalking typically occurs during:**
   A) REM sleep
   B) Stage 1 of non-REM sleep
   C) Stage 3 or 4 of non-REM sleep
   D) Transition between REM and wakefulness

9- C,	10- B,	11- B,	12- B,	13- B,	14- C,	15- C

Notes -

Notes -

Notes -

www.ingramcontent.com/pod-product-compliance
Lightning Source LLC
Chambersburg PA
CBHW041732100726
47973CB00011B/187

9798896998891